can I Believe in miracles?

Ralph L. Murray

BROADMAN PRESS
Nashville, Tennessee

DEWEY DECIMAL CLASSIFICATION NUMBER: 226.7
Library of Congress catalog card number: 67-22031
Printed in the United States of America
5.F6713

Contents

1 The Witness of the Miracles

John 20:30-31

If I were to ask, "Do you believe in the miracles of Jesus?" most of you would reply: "Why, certainly. I believe he healed the sick, walked on the water, raised the dead, turned the water to wine, and all the rest. It never occurred to me *not* to believe in them."

Without realizing it, that last grand affirmation exposes the weakness that may bring down the house of your own faith. For sooner or later, disbelieving the miracles will occur to you, not as an academic question, but as a desperately personal one.

Suppose you were urged to defend the miracles in the Gospel stories. What would you say? Perhaps you would stammer out something about their being in the Bible, and that you believe the Bible. Or you might mumble something about their being a part of Jesus' life and ministry; or, it might be that for the first time you would honestly ask, Does one truly have to believe the miracles to be a Christian?

There are several ways of taking the miracle stories, and one of them will probably find most of us. We may confine the miraculous to a special and unique era. In this we assume that miracles belong to the never-to-be-repeated New Testament situation. Reflect on the story of the fishing trip made by three clergymen of differing faiths. Once out in the boat, one remembered a favorite lure he had left on the shore. Without ceremony, he walked over the water and got it. The second man of the cloth, not to be outdone, used the same method to retrieve his lunch from the car. The third, convinced that his own credentials were at stake, on some pretext stepped out of the boat onto the water and promptly sank like a rock. When he had been hauled back into the boat, the first clergyman turned to the second and asked, "Do you suppose we should show our friend here where the rocks are?"

1

Beyond the obvious humor of this story is the quiet assumption that the day of miracles is long since past—if, indeed, it ever was. It is absurd to think about a man's walking on the water, unless he be a young daredevil who waterskis barefoot!

Another way of looking at the miracles is to assume that somewhere there is a perfectly natural explanation for them and sooner or later we will stumble onto it. Still another way is to regard them simply as lovely stories to neither believe nor disbelieve. We only observe that it is a pity God is not as active as he used to be. And if we are sophisticated enough, we may go on to say that these miracle stories certainly credit the faith of the writers.

The end result of all such efforts to make the miracle stories palatable lowers a depth charge in our psyches that is ticking away toward a bone-shaking concussion. If something is not done to detonate the charge it will go off some day and blow our faith sky-high, and prayer will go with it. For, after all, prayer is related (however tightly or loosely) to the possibility of the miraculous. If we have no real faith in miracles, we get more and more shaky about the worth of prayer.

So rises the conviction that we have something more in these miracles than an interesting body of material to be read and appreciated much like the fairy tales of our childhood. These are an integral part of the ministry and teaching of Jesus; they have something important to do with his mission and message. If we understand them and accept them, strong is our faith. If not, we have a weak seam that is going to give way.

How shall we take these miracles? We could start with the miracles themselves: make a careful, detailed study of the world view of the New Testament; of the objective documentation available; the reportorial method; the internal evidence. But when we got through we would still have the question unanswered.

Forget the miracles for a moment; look rather at the men who wrote about them. What kind of men were they?

There are three things we may say about these men. First, they knew that God is not understood apart from his acts of grace and power. Second, they were convinced that God had acted in Jesus Christ. And third, there is an interrelationship of miracles and faith.

The God Who Acts

The men of the Bible are not given to abstractions; they do not find God at the end of a syllogism; they find him in their own hearts. They experience him, and this is the clue that helps them know what God is like. For the Bible does not know God apart from what he does. And the first thing the Bible men know about God is that he loves. Sometimes he is pictured as a loving husband (Hos. 2:14-16); sometimes as a solicitous father (Hos. 11:1); sometimes as a deliverer (Deut. 26:7-8). But always he is known by what he does. He raises up a Moses or a Joshua, a Samuel or a David. He delivers the Hebrews from the Egyptians.

These holy men of old saw God presiding in a sovereign freedom over both nature and history. Neither was a closed system. God was not limited; neither was he capricious. He was too good to devise mischief; too wise to do wrong.

When we come to the New Testament it is no different. God acts in a different way, to be sure, but he acts. He comes as a baby in a manger; he lives among men; he talks their language; he sorts truth from error. And in the course of this life he runs afoul the vested interests of religious men and their institutions. He who is sinless (and has no ax to grind) is thrown into the grinding wheels of the establishment and comes out writhing on a barbarous Roman cross. But his claim to be the unique Son of God (understood by friend and foe alike) seems to be lost in the agony of that hapless death. Sorrowfully, some who had loved him best laid him away. It was ironic that such a noble life should come to such an ignoble end. Faith was driven to the wall.

But in that dark night of the soul God acted, and the next chapter tells of a resurrection. Those whose faith had been stretched on the rack of death came back to boldly declare that in the events of this one life there is a saving gospel; that even this gospel has something of the power of God.

So these men of the Bible trace out what God has done— both in the world at large and in the inner world of their own hearts. They know what God is like, because they know what he has done for them. This is where we must begin, if we are to understand the witness of the miracles.

God in Christ

Beyond the tender story of Bethlehem and the manger, the brave life of Jesus, the brutal death, and the authenticating resurrection is this one claim—"God was in Christ, reconciling the world unto himself" (2 Cor. 5:19).

What is this, if not a miracle? Before we ever get to the miracle stories, we are confronted by a miracle: a man in whom God is found. Can we believe this miracle?

When we come down to the heart of it, we are facing a question of identity: Who is this Jesus? Whose side is he on?

The Bible takes great pains to tell us that Jesus stands on our side; that he is fully and wholly human. It is interesting that the first heresies denied this. They said Jesus could not be fully and wholly human. But this is exactly what the Bible asserts.

The whole life of Jesus on earth becomes unreal to us unless we understand that it was truly a *human* life. Jesus was first a baby, then a boy, then a man. When He was a boy, He had to learn things gradually as other boys had to do. And when He was a man he knew no more in scientific and historical matters than other men of His time. He did not know in advance, each moment, everything that was going to happen. He often had to go forward, as it were, in the dark, walking by faith, and it was sometimes very difficult. Even more important, He had to fight real battles against temptation, as all men have to do. They were not sham fights, but real conflicts, and sometimes terribly hard ones.[1]

So Jesus was completely human. But to be completely human means to be *perfectly* human. All the bad in us is a *perversion* of our humanity. It is not that Jesus falls short of being fully human; it is that *we* do. We are the ones who have fallen. We are the ones who lose the battle with temptation. Jesus stands on our side.

The Bible also tells us that Jesus stands on God's side. Paul's great epistle to the Colossians pictures the Christ as standing on God's side in creation, in redemption, as the head of the church, which is his body (cf. Col. 1:13 to 2:5). And when we move out beyond the brackets of human history, Christ will be standing with God.

Here we stumble on the thought that Christianity itself rests on a miracle. Here is Jesus, standing with man—limited, confined, torn by conflict and temptation. But he also stands with God—infinite, eternal, complete. This is a miracle far greater than walking on the water.

Faith and Miracle

Now how can we accept this?

As we look at the men who reported the miracles, there was one thing they had in common; and that is the miracle of the indwelling Christ. Before ever a miracle was written down there was this prior miracle of experiencing Christ within. And that miracle begins with faith, saving faith. This is our clue.

What was true with them is true with us. We have sensed this chasm between ourselves and God. It is a chasm of incompleteness, of guilt, of mortality. And on our side of the chasm Christ comes, speaking to our incompleteness, our guilt, our mortality. At last we take courage and look across this chasm. There, on the other side Christ also stands. And in shame for what we are, we gaze in wonder upon him. In that moment the chasm disappears, and the miracle of the new birth has taken place.

What was the sequence? Was it from miracle to faith? No. It was from faith to miracle. The *eyes of faith* "see" the miracle, and the miracle confirms faith.

The witness of the miracles, then, is not a witness that would bring us to faith. Not that. It is a witness that confirms faith. If there is no faith, then miracles and signs and wonders are unbelievable.

Graham Greene has a powerful play called *The Potting Shed*. As the story begins, Henry Callifer is dying. All the members of the family have been summoned to his bedside except his son James. When James arrives, he pleads with his mother to be allowed to see his father, but she will not allow it. It is the same as always—shut out, treated like an outcast. He cannot understand why he should be cut off so, and he determines to find out. After his father's funeral he learns from his uncle, the Reverend William Callifer (who is also a priest), that once in his boyhood he—James—had hanged himself in the garden potting shed. When the gardener found him he was dead; his heart had stopped beating; there was no sign of life. But his uncle prayed over him, and just as surely as he had been dead, so he became alive: his pulse returned, his breathing began, he rose up, conscious of all around him. But his father, who was a renowned and famous freethinker, had written many books debunking faith; exploding the illusion of the miraculous; discounting prayer. To admit the reality of what had happened in the potting shed would mean the supreme embarrassment of all he had come to stand for. It was easier to deny the existence of his own son. So the father, in order that he might deny faith, denied the miracle that took place in his own potting shed. For him the son continued dead.

In a small way Greene casts us a light. If we understand the miracles, we must begin with the resurrection. If we deny the reality of that, or if we have never known it, then what difference do the miracles make? For the witness of the miracles is a witness to a living faith.

Now this is not theology only, it is history. For a man did rise from the dead (a miracle) and appeared to a number of people who had known him during his earthly life. It is significant that he appeared only to those who were his friends: to Mary in the garden, to the two disciples on the Emmaus Road, to the eleven in the upper room, to Peter by the seashore, and to certain others. He never did stride into the Jewish Sanhedrin, or the soldier's barracks, or the governor's palace. He came to his friends; to those who believed in him.

The miracle of the resurrection witnessed to them—to their faith, which lay bruised and battered on the ground of their hearts. Then they looked back and saw that the past months were literally strewn with miracles: miracles to believe; miracles to preach and report; miracles to sustain faith in other dark hours that were still to come. For these miracles witnessed and confirmed their surmise that God (who moves in power) is like a father, and that his acts are wrought in love.

Is it different with us?

Notes

1. D. M. Baillie, *Out of Nazareth* (New York: Charles Scribner's Sons, 1958), p. 162. Used by permission.

2 Demons Go to Church

Mark 1:23-28

Our Scripture passage opens on a familiar scene: An assembled congregation is in its place of worship. The speaker of the hour is about to conclude his remarks; a certain restlessness registers here and there. Not the restlessness of boredom but of resistance. With an uncanny perceptiveness the speaker has moved beyond the shallow platitudes, so familiar in the church, to the rough and tumble of daily life. With an unfailing skill, he has made faith something more than a tired tradition. He has made it a lively jousting with the known and the familiar moods, thoughts, and emotions that flow in and out through daily life.

Suddenly the resistance breaks out into the open. A man cries out: " 'What have you to do with us, Jesus of Nazareth? Have you come to destroy us?' " (Mark 1:24, RSV).

The most natural thing in the world is to begin to ask questions. This is how Mark introduces the public ministry of the Saviour. He is writing from a particular point of view—that of faith—but what is he saying? Does this story have anything to say to us today? In our quest for an answer, let me propose four approaches: the sequence; the setting; the subject; and finally the surrender.

The Sequence

If we could approach Mark's Gospel with fresh eyes—discarding all familiarity with the stories and even the phrases—we would be far more likely to examine the structure of the author's work. Were we to make such an examination, we would be delightfully surprised to uncover the literary finesse, the drama, and the skill with which Mark wrote, forgetting that he had no pattern for his Gospel. He was blazing a new trail; he was the first to take the freely shifting elements of the remembered events in the

7

life of Jesus and give them a literary shape, a structure, a movement with design. And, of course, behind the form is the divine
purpose.

Does it surprise you that this joust with the demon came right
after Jesus' baptism and the temptations, right at the beginning
of his public life? Could it be that Mark is telling us that Christianity (in whatever form it may come) will never win by de-
fault? The powers of evil are implacable, vigilant, alert.

Almost any Christian will recognize the truth which lies so
quietly in the structure Mark gives the story. We no sooner begin
the Christian life than the powers of evil launch an intensified
attack. In his delightful little work *The Screwtape Letters,* C. S.
Lewis composed some imaginative letters to a junior devil whose
name is Wormwood. Wormwood has been assigned a "patient" by
Screwtape; the "patient" shortly becomes a Christian. In his second letter, Screwtape writes Wormwood:

MY DEAR WORMWOOD:

I note with grave displeasure that your patient has become a
Christian. . . . There is no need to despair; hundreds of these adult
converts have been reclaimed after a brief sojourn in the Enemy's
camp and are now with us. All the *habits* of the patient, both mental
and bodily, are still in our favour.[1]

Professor Lewis quite properly recognized that becoming a Christian does not lessen the attacks of the devil; they are intensified.
All our old thought-sets and physical habits are mobilized against
us. He mentions in the course of the letters some of the avenues
of attack: the contradictions in the church, prayer life, worldly
friends, physical pleasures, the pocketbook, sex, domestic preoccupation.

What is it Lewis is doing in these whimsical letters? Writing
solely to entertain us? No, not that. In his foreword he inti-
mates his purpose: "The best way to drive out the devil, if he
will not yield to texts of Scripture, is to jeer and flout him, for
he cannot bear scorn." Through the use of whimsy and
imagination, Professor Lewis is telling us that we can expect an
intensified attack whenever we become serious about the matter
of being a Christian.

The Setting

The encounter of our story took place in the synagogue of Capernaum. The people involved were first-century people, with first-century ideas about reality. And one of the things that was very real to all of them was the idea of demons. It may sound fantastic to us, but to those in the story, demons were very real. Even the medical testbooks of the time took demons seriously. One has been discovered that includes a formula for the exorcising of demons in the preparation of medicine. The ancient people believed demons were waiting and watching for an opportunity to do mischief.

Harnack describes the terror of the times: "The whole world and the circumambient atmosphere were filled with devils; not merely idolatry, but every phase and form of life were ruled by them. They sat on thrones, they hovered around cradles. The world was literally a hell."[2] In ancient burial places skulls have been found that were trepanned or had a small hole bored in them. Without benefit of anesthetic or surgical instrument, this formidable operation was performed and undergone to release demons through the hole in the skull.

The question of whether or not Jesus believed in demons misses the point altogether. *The people did,* and in this form the forces of darkness had blown a withering blast across Jesus' world. The encounter that day in the Capernaum synagogue was between Jesus and the whole terrifying, haunted, intact world. The real question is this: Who has the final power? Mark proceeds to answer with this story.

Evil today clothes itself differently. We may not believe in demons, but we must believe in the power of the devil. It is everywhere. It is in business. A lawyer said to a business friend not long ago: "To make out in the business world today my boy should be trained in jungle warfare." Men may not believe in demons in our sophisticated day, but in their pursuit of money and the power that brings money, they act like demons.

Evil has another face in our modern setting. It is sex. Not the gift that God gave for use within the framework of marriage, but sex as a symbol, a device, an outlet, an expression, an exploitation. Thinking through the setting in which we must live out our Christian lives, in which we must conduct our own battle with the forces of evil, my eyes swept across the jumble of resource materials that inevitably goes with writing. Fairly jumping off the front cover of one magazine was the bold question, "What's happening to sex in America?"[3] It was a frank treatment of this part of our way of life. Then my eye caught the front page of a secular publication. In one corner was an announcement of a feature article in that issue: "Teen-age Movies and Morals."[4] In a six-page spread, profusely illustrated with bikini-clad teen-age girls, the article purported to support the idea that the surfing-swimming-necking crowds of today were really puritans at heart. This is hard to believe, especially when statistics are known.

Also among the papers, books, and articles on my desk was the current copy of *Christianity Today,* featuring an editorial titled "Shattering the American Image." It was a description of illicit sex practices by the American soldier abroad. It is hard to believe that 90 percent of the GIs indulge "more or less frequently" in illicit sex. One of the soldiers wrote of the practice of his fellow soldiers to "own" a girl:

"The soldier lives with the girl during his off-duty time. . . . When he leaves Korea, he 'sells' her to a newcomer. If he is broke, he may 'rent' her out to others. Under such circumstances, of course, venereal disease is as common as a cold in the head. Forty percent of the troops serving in Korea during a year will get VD. A young boy may be horrified the first time this happens to him, but he is kidded out of his shock, and often becomes a repeater who never learns and ceases to care."[5]

Could I share one more small piece of evidence? It was a letter written to Molly Mayfield, the news column counselor:

DEAR MRS. MAYFIELD:

My husband travels on his job and is gone three weeks out of four. I have two children and keep busy during the day but the nights are miserable.

About a month ago I was feeling pretty low when a man I'd met a couple of weeks before called and asked if he could come over. I said it was all right. I guess I knew it was bound to lead to trouble and now I think I'm pregnant. I'm not sure it isn't my husband's but there is doubt.

Shall I tell my husband "all" and hope he doesn't leave and take the children or shall I keep it all within myself? There is no one I can confide in, and I don't think I can live the rest of my life with this on my mind. Every time I look at the baby I'll remember my horrible mistake—I'll have a constant reminder.

What can I do? I'm about to lose my mind.

SUNK[6]

What is the point of all this? Like Jesus we are not engaged in conflict with a paper tiger. The setting is real; the temptations and the struggles make the pulse pound and the nerves tingle. Demons are demons whether of the first-century variety or the twentieth.

The Subject

We might have thought Jesus would have been annoyed to have his message interrupted as it was. But not so. More important than the message was the man. Like Kipling's M'Andrew, Jesus' central question was always, What about the man?

This man had fallen under the influence of the demons of his day; he was in their grip, even as many of us are today. He was something less than God had intended. Divided, torn, a civil war going on in his head, the quiet authority of Jesus seemed to set the whole thing going again.

Since man is the most important of all the Father's concerns, and since the heart of Jesus beats with the heart of the Father, he focused his concern on this one man; on his needs.

If you have a civil war going on inside your head and heart, you can take courage from this. In some quiet way the Father will come to you, if only you let him. Francis Thompson was one of the greatest of English poets, but there was a time when he was literally a homeless beggar, with broken boots and no shirt beneath his coat. Tramping the streets of London, starving and sleeping nights on the embankment, he never forgot a certain Mr. M'Master, a shoemaker of Panton Street in London. One night when he was frozen with cold, when he was sick with hunger, when his head was spinning with weakness, a hand was laid on his shoulder. It was this Mr. M'Master. "Is your soul saved?" said Mr. M'Master. Francis Thompson was a proud man,

even when he was starving. "What right have you," he blazed
out, "to ask me that question?" "Ah, well," said M'Master, "if
you won't let me save your soul, let me save your body!" He
took Francis Thompson home with him and gave him food and
shelter and work to do. That was the first step; eventually Francis
Thompson was soundly converted.

Men who are divided, who are at war with themselves, are
lost men. And our Saviour said, "The Son of man is come to
seek and to save that which was lost" (Luke 19:10).

The Surrender

We can be quite sure that in his best moments this demon-
ridden man hated himself. But he had never gotten the upper
hand; his dark impulses were more than he could master—until that
day when Jesus spoke peace.

The point of the miracle is not that Jesus was a wonder-worker.
Here was power; here was authority. This was the power of God
challenging the powers of darkness, and coming off first and best.
And the wonder of it for Mark was that when any man invites the
Spirit of Christ into his heart, that man has an ally who must
win the victory—even over death.

To understand the point Mark was making, we must recall
that this was written long years after Mark had become a Christian. He is looking back, along with the whole young Christian
community, on these miracles which Jesus did, and looking with
the eyes of faith. As he looks, it dawns on him that this miracle
bore a witness about Jesus that even the unlearned, secular-minded
peasants recognized. What was that witness? Martin Luther has
put it into verse:

> Did we in our own strength confide,
>   Our striving would be losing;
> Were not the right Man on our side,
>   The Man of God's own choosing:

> Dost ask who that may be?
>   Christ Jesus, it is He;
> Lord Sabaoth, His name,
>   From age to age the same,
> And He must win the battle.

Notes

1. C. S. Lewis, *The Screwtape Letters* (N. Y.: The Macmillan Co., 1961), p. 15.

2. A. Harnack, *The Expansion of Christianity,* I, 161.

3. *Guideposts,* July, 1964.

4. *Look,* November 3, 1964, pp. 60-64.

5. *Christianity Today,* October 23, 1964, p. 26. Copyright 1964 by Christianity Today. Used by permission.

6. *The Knoxville News-Sentinel,* October 6, 1964. Used by permission of United Feature Syndicate, New York.

3 A Private Miracle
Mark 1:29-31

The Scripture story before us is immediately preceded by an hour at the synagogue. Now worship is over, and Simon Peter goes to his home. He steps from the sublime, rapturous hour of inspiration and prayer back into the familiar world of unrealized dreams, unravelled plans, unfulfilled hopes, and dreary tasks. When he returns home from church, trouble meets him at the front door. His wife's mother is sick with a burning fever.

Now there is no miracle in that. It is all too familiar. This is the world we know so well. But there is a miracle here. It is introduced by the little word "they." When Simon Peter went home from church, he took Jesus with him. Jesus went with Peter into the drab, commonplace world where Peter spent his days. And what follows might be called the private miracle.

That is what most of us need—a private miracle. It is not the great occasions that wear us down; it is the daily routine. Mark speaks to the need we all feel in this brief account before us. With an unobtrusive art he brings to focus the setting, the symbol, and the service of this private miracle.

The Setting: A Private Home

The gift for setting forth the essential features of the story is reflected in the very first sentence: "Forthwith, when they were come out of the synagogue, they entered into the house of Simon" (1:29). This is the setting for this private miracle.

We are not surprised by little miracles that occur in church; in fact, we faintly expect them.

Nor are we surprised at the thought of a miracle in the great world around us. Formerly we thought of the world of nature as a closed system. Even God was fenced out of nature; the thought of a possible miracle brought a knowing smile. But now science has taught us reverence. Even the smallest particle of

14

matter (they tell us) is alive with motion. Nature is not a closed, rigid, and fixed system; it is open, and free, and fluid. We have been taught a certain humility as we approach the natural world, sensing that there are more things in heaven and earth than are dreamed of in our philosophy. Even the idea of miracles in the great world finds hospitality with us. After all, we live with broken atoms, supersonic speed, and Tel-star. As for miracles in the world of nature, we can believe almost anything.

Could it be that Mark is quietly telling us here that miracles can overtake us anywhere? It can happen on Monday as well as Sunday; at home as well as at church? All a private miracle requires is a needy person and an adequate Saviour. The rest is variable.

Headed for a meeting, several minutes late, I paused on the steps of the building to ask a young preacher friend, "How is it with you?"

Quite honestly he replied, "Bad. Very bad."

I turned aside with him, and we talked perhaps for twenty minutes. It was a familiar story—strife and factionalism in his congregation; charges and countercharges; people for and people against. And the young preacher in the middle. "I'm going to resign," he said.

With four children to feed, no place to live, and less than a week's salary in the bank, a man—even a preacher—has to be pretty desperate to adopt a course of action like that. Since there was not anything I could do at the moment, we had a brief prayer and went on in to the meeting.

As we sat down together, a Negro man stood up to sing. His voice was like a magnificent organ—volume that could make the windows rattle or soften down to the lyric quality of the flute.

When your enemies assail, and your heart begins to fail,
   Don't forget that God in heaven answers prayer;
He will make a way for you and will lead you safely through;
   Take your burden to the Lord and leave it there.

Then came the chorus, sung with such depth of feeling, such freedom of spirit, such sincerity, that it seemed he was singing only to us.

I looked over at my young preacher friend. The lines of

anxious care were smoothed out, and on his face was a look of peace. His eyes were moist as I leaned over and whispered, "Your Father in heaven has just sent you a message." He nodded his head.

That was a private miracle. The only ones who knew were the young preacher, the Father in heaven, and myself. Not even the singer knew. Here again was a quiet assurance that a miracle can happen anytime.

The Symbol: A fever

Most of the miracles the Gospel writers tell us about have a certain desperation in them—men blind, lame, paralyzed, demon-possessed; children and servants at the point of death. As we reflect on the skill and art of the writer of Mark, it dawns on us there is nothing desperate about this case; it is only a fever. He is assuring us that Jesus not only has power for the mortal sickness that darkens our days but that he also has power for the feverish piques and moods that mark our ways.

Life today is a feverish affair for many of us. Our natural and right desires all too often become fevers—amusement fevers; sports fevers; pleasure fevers; ambition fevers; work fevers; feeling fevers. We permit them to get all out of bounds and balance. Life is shot through with frictions and tensions which are involved in the mere business of living with our families, our business associates, our friends.

Fevers are an integral part of life—any life—and we may as well stop looking across the fence to greener pastures. The problem is not a particular job nor a unique set of circumstances, though some are more trying than others. The problem is everywhere.

Could it be that within our own hearts is the seat of the fever? Often we find that the feverish rounds that tie us up in knots begin not with the morning of every new day but with what we think is important. What we need is not a new schedule but a new scheme. The thing that needs rearranging is our system of values. We need to make room for the important things.

> If you place your nose on the grindstone rough
> And keep it down there long enough,

> You'll soon forget there are such things
> As brooks that babble and birds that sing;
> And as for you, your whole world will compose
> Just you, the stone, and your ground-down nose.[1]

This brief parable which Mark includes very early in his story tells us that Jesus wants to be of service in the midst of our everyday worries, needs, and fevers. Perhaps here is one of the meanings of that lovely story John told when Jesus washed the feet of the disciples (13:1-11). He only washed their feet, you will recall, and refused the bath Peter wanted. It was the dust from the journey Jesus wanted to cleanse away. Many of us have been bathed by Jesus; we have received his cleansing and salvation from the dark guilt of sin. What we need is the cleansing of our feet as we walk life's daily journey. Jesus wants to serve us by constantly washing away the grime and cooling the fever of our ordinary days.

Lew Wallace, in his novel *Ben Hur,* puts in the mouth of his hero a truth that we have all observed in life: the race is not always to the swift, nor is it always to the strong. Sometimes the race belongs to those who have learned how to keep down the fevers.

Paul Tournier, the great Swiss Christian doctor, writes of visiting an old pastor who knew how to handle life's fevers. Praying was one of his common remedies. The physician could never conclude a visit without a prayer from the old man. Moreover, it seemed that the pastor's prayers were just a continuation of an intimate conversation that had been momentarily suspended. William Barclay, in *The Gospel of Mark,* quotes Dr. Tournier after one such visit as saying:

[I went home and] talked it over with my wife, and together we asked God to give us also the close fellowship with Jesus the old pastor had. Since then He has been the center of my devotion and my travelling companion. He takes pleasure in what I do, and concerns himself with it. He is a friend with whom I can discuss everything that happens in my life. He shares my joy and my pain, my hopes and my fears. He is there when a patient speaks to me from his heart, listening to him with me and better than I can. And when the patient is gone I can talk to him about it.[2]

The Task: Service to Others

When Jesus entered the very ordinary little home, he found the household schedule upset by illness. The mother-in-law lay sick with a fever. Jesus did not seem to see the disorder in the home; he saw the disorder in the life of this woman. Taking her by the hand, Jesus banished the fever from her. Once the fever was broken, once Jesus had ministered to her need, she immediately plunged into the task of ministering to him. It was a rather commonplace task, even prosaic; she prepared a meal. She was in a key position to do a needed task, and that was enough. She went right to work. She who had been ministered unto began to minister.

Is it not a little sad that we instinctively wait around for someone else to do what obviously needs to be done? That we have a strong impulse to save ourselves, to hold something back in reserve?

If this story serves no other purpose than to inspire us to do a task that obviously needs to be done, it has become for us a sure word from the Lord.

> Let none hear you idly saying,
>   "There is nothing I can do,"
> While the souls of men are dying,
>   And the Master calls for you;
> Take the task He gives you gladly;
>   Let His work your pleasure be;
> Answer quickly when He calleth,
>   "Here am I, send me, send me."[3]

Mountain Doctor is a book about a physician who has given a good part of his life to a selfless professional service to the mountain people of Transylvania County, North Carolina. At a little settlement called Balsam Grove, Dr. Cannon has built a hospital and clinic, using the labor of his mountain friends, the materials that nature provides, and the money that he has earned from his own modest fees.

To anyone curious enough to ask why a modern medical doctor would bury himself in such a remote, harsh, demanding situation, a rather surprising answer will emerge.

One day while I was interning, still adrift as far as my religious experience was concerned and quite unhappy about it, I happened to pick up a little magazine, and in it I discovered an article titled "The Jungle Doctor." I began reading it casually, but I quickly became interested.

That was in 1931. Then he tells how this jungle doctor, Dr. Schweitzer of Europe and Africa, began to have a profound influence on his own feverish way of life.

"As I began to be deeply concerned about other people . . . and about my search to find a way out of doubt and despair into confidence and hope and peace, I began to feel this doubt and darkness lifting and light and peace calming my troubled thoughts. This then, I told myself, is what I want, what I need, what I have been searching for. . . . Some persons have defined it as the essence of Christianity, as the way of life of Jesus of Galilee, and it seems to me that it is. But however that may be, it sustains me."[4]

So this story comes to us across the mountains—as Mark comes across the centuries—and speaks to our feverish, frenzied, hectic lives. Jesus has a private miracle for us, if we will let him give it. That miracle might be described by words once dropped from the lips of the great preacher of Boston, Phillips Brooks: "Do not pray for tasks equal to your powers. Pray for powers equal to your tasks! Then the doing of your work shall be no miracle, but you shall be a miracle. Every day you will wonder at yourself, at the richness of life that has come to you by the grace of God."

Notes

1. Rotary Letter, May, 1957.

2. William Barclay, *The Gospel of Mark* (The Daily Bible Study Series, Philadelphia: The Westminster Press, 1957, U.S.A.), p. 30. Used by permission.

3. Daniel March, "Hark, the Voice of Jesus Calling," *Baptist Hymnal* (Nashville: Convention Press, 1956), p. 440.

4. LeGette Blythe, *Mountain Doctor* (New York: William Morrow & Co., 1964), pp. 60-61. Copyright 1964 by LeGette Blythe. Used by permission.

4 The Untouchables
Mark 1:40-45

This vivid story of the leper contains all the elements Mark wants to weave into his Gospel at this point: a hopeless sufferer, the hapless priests, the helpless religious establishment; and in contrast the warm, infinitely tender and mighty Saviour. This story helps fill out the picture of Jesus as Mark wants us to see him.

Most of us know nothing of leprosy. We have never had it; we have never known anyone who had it. Leprosy is no threat to us.

But it was a threat to Mark's first readers. Leprosy was about the dirtiest trick life could play on a man. No other disease could touch it for sheer agony mixed with horror. It would strike a small spot on the skin and begin its deadly work. Even the victim might not know until the dreaded numbness set in, or the open sore refused to heal, or the body began to cover itself with the telltale white scales. The seige of terror once begun, advanced slowly: finger by finger, or feature by feature, finally erasing the whole human face, leaving behind a messy trail of scabs, scales, and running sores. And it would keep on rotting flesh and bone as long as there was any life. The white sheet the leper wore was the burial shroud of a living corpse.

Beyond the grim physical horror was the moral and spiritual burden leprosy attached to its victim. It was the dirty sign of God's condemnation. Leprosy was the devil's vilest practical joke. The affliction of the leper was the mark of Cain in its darkest sense. Lepers were isolated without the dignity of prison bars or the security of a warden's care.

Before such a scourge the priests were helpless. Healing a leper was mentioned in the same breath with raising the dead. The whole religious establishment was mocked by one leper, and since they could not help him, they banished him. They even had a ritual for it (cf. Lev. 13:46).

This is the background we must keep in mind as we read these five brief verses. Mark would have us understand something about this Jesus of Nazareth. He is etching out for us a profile of his wonderful Saviour, whose coming and whose presence has taken the empty forms of religion and filled them with saving grace and power.

If you read the story closely, you will stumble on three miracles in its brief compass. There is the miracle of relationship; then the miracle of love; and finally, the miracle we anticipate—the miracle of power.

A Miracle of Relationship

Mark starts the story with the simple statement: "There came a leper to him" (1:40). That in itself comprises a small miracle. So complete was the isolation of a leper's life—as prescribed by Old Testament religious law—as to make him a human derelict. One rabbi of Jesus' time boasted that he always flung stones at lepers to keep them away. Other religious teachers, not quite so unfeeling, confessed they hid themselves or took to their heels whenever a leper appeared, even in the distance. That a leper would have courage to approach any teacher—even Jesus—is a miracle.

Despair was the hallmark of the leper. He was the original Lonesome George. He had to stay out of touch; most times out of sight; always out of pocket. He was a cell of concentrated anguish—moving, scrounging, hiding. He had nothing more than his miserable and daily existence.

Relationship—even the simplest kind—was next to impossible. The best he could expect was an averted glance and a stepped-up pace.

For some of us it is not too difficult to imagine this terrible sense of isolation, this imposed loneliness that the leper felt. Although we have no physical leprosy on our bodies, we carry the internal marks of the outcast—loneliness. We have the same sullen and exaggerated spirit of independence. Not having known any real friendship, we are unfriendly. We know what it is to be alone while near the crowd; to have acquaintances, but no friends; to be in a house, but not at home.

This alienation sometimes keeps us from coming to church;

sometimes it *keeps* us coming, in faint hope. It makes us hold our brother at arm's length; spurn his overtures as an invasion of privacy. The mask we wear smiles and nods and says all the right things, but when we get alone in our bedroom and take the mask off, an insuppressible sigh escapes us. It is such a relief!

These experiences afford a faint glimmering of the internal barrier the leper had to leap when he approached Jesus. He must have hoped for better treatment from Jesus than he could expect from any of the religious establishment—priest, scribe, or Levite.

Institutional religion repulsed him; but not Jesus.

Is the institutional religion of today any better?

Churches as institutions find themselves firmly rooted in a cultural setting, with values, ways of looking at things, built-in contradictions. Their membership is made up of people who are influenced and shaped by the world in which they live, from which, like the plants and trees of the forest, they draw their very life. The local church, shaped as it is by these nonchurch forces, is confronted by demands that set our very teeth on edge. Here another drummer beats; another piper pipes. And it sounds strange in our ears.

The call is to go against the grain, not only the grain of the familiar, even comfortable, world around us, but the grain of our own inclinations, drives, dreams. So what do we do? We water it all down; clip off an edge here and there; temporize and rationalize. Then some poor moral leper comes along whose sheer desperation calls for something drastic and different, and our anemic remedies will not help. So what do we do? What we are compelled to do: either ignore him or banish him.

It is no wonder Dietrich Bonhoeffer in his Flossenberg prison cell called for "religionless Christianity."[1] Or that the dour Kierkegaard would all but reject the churches of his native Denmark nearly a century ago:

Denmark has fallen so low religiously that it is not only lower than anything hitherto seen of Christianity but lower than Jewry, in fact it can only be compared to the lowest forms of paganism—to such a degree have people forgotten the point in Christianity: self-denial, while worldly well-being and soft-hearted mediocrity are idolised.[2]

In our nervous desire to protect ourselves and our interests—and I indict myself here—we can obscure Jesus, who is the very heartbeat of all we try to do.

One of the most revolutionary devotional books of this century is Charles Sheldon's *In His Steps*. You recall the story: a young man decides to live for thirty days with the earnest question, What would Jesus do? In working out his answers to that recurring question in his daily affairs, he revolutionizes himself and the community where he lives and works. It is an interesting, absorbing story; but it is more. It is a disarming protest against obscuring the Jesus of Nazareth in our fainthearted efforts to secure our beloved and historic institutions against the ire of prejudice and vested interests.

The first miracle was that the leper sensed something in Jesus that encouraged him to overcome his natural inhibitions; his learned hesitations. No congregation has truly learned of Christ until it has developed a fellowship that has this drawing, attractive power: the power to establish a meaningful relationship.

A Miracle of Love

The second sentence literally jumps out at us when we read this familiar story again: "Jesus, moved with compassion, put forth his hand, and touched him" (v. 41).

Did it occur to you that Jesus felt no threat in this leper—none at all? He did not throw rocks; he did not run; he did not even stall for time. He met the challenge head-on.

One of the more recent translations of Mark's story reads: "Jesus, moved with warm indignation." What was it that made Jesus indignant—the approach of the leper, the interruption of a sermon, being put on the spot?

It was no unworthy thing like that. We must remember that Jesus saw his whole ministry cast as a conflict against the powers of darkness. Jesus had come to lead men out into the light: men who were in bondage; men who had been beaten to a pulp; men who were burdened beyond function. The thought that stirred Jesus to indignation could well have been the terrible and pitiable plight of this one, poor creature, so completely in the bondage of evil. This one leper was a symbol of every leper, not only physical, but moral and spiritual as well.

The devil was baiting the Saviour. Jesus rose to the challenge. He reached out and touched him!

So far, this is nothing more than a sentimental historic remembrance. The thing that concerns us is how all this can touch us in our fouled-up, complicated situation. The devil can tie us up in so many different ways—an impossible work situation; an intolerable domestic relationship; family; a moral weakness. "Is there any hope for me?" you ask. "Can Jesus touch me?"

In answer I would challenge you to hold in your heart one tremendous thought, straight from the New Testament: "He is the head of the body, the church"(Col. 1:18). This disarmingly simple statement declares that our Lord still has a living, breathing, functioning physical body in the world, and that is his church.

This means that through the church the Saviour can touch your life—mixed up, snarled, and confused—in marvellous, comforting, and healing ways. Without suggesting any sacramental significance at all, let me affirm that the deep inner guilt you feel may be touched as you enter the waters of baptism—the waters the New Testament calls "the washing of regeneration" (Titus 3:5). Or you may find a calm, sweet sense of serenity possessing you as in the communion with the body and blood of our Lord you yield yourself anew to the Saviour (1 Cor. 10:16). Or, a definite sense of this healing touch may come quite simply in the touch of a fellow Christian.

Alexander Irving, in *My Lady of the Chimney Corner,* has a beautiful passage in which he shows us the touch of the Saviour can stream through a consecrated personality. "The lady" goes to comfort a neighbor whose boy lies dead. After a brief conversation, in which the grief-stricken mother pleads for some token that God is with her in her distress, Anna has the bereaved kneel beside her bed, indicating that God will touch her with his hand. And then Irving continues:

As gently as falls an autumn leaf, she laid her hand on Eliza's head: "Ah, wuman, God isn't a printed book to be carried around by a man in fine clothes, not a gold cross to be danglin' at the watchchain of a priest. God's Spirit comes in as many ways as there's need fur it comin', and that's quite a when . . . God takes a hand wherever He can find it, and jist does what He likes with it. Sometimes He takes

a Bishop's hand and lays it on a child's head in benediction, then
He takes the hand of a doctor to relieve pain, the hand of a mother
to guide a chile, and sometimes He takes the hand of a poo old
craither like me to give comfort to a neighbor. But they're all hands
touched by His Spirit, and His Spirit is everywhere lukin' for hands
to use."[3]

> 'Tis the human touch in this world that counts,
>   The touch of your hand and mine,
> Which means far more to the fainting heart,
>   Than shelter and bread and wine;
> For shelter is gone when the night is o'er,
>   And bread lasts only a day,
> But the touch of a hand and the sound of a voice
>   Sing on in the soul alway.[4]

The Miracle of Power

The rest of this brief story relates to the cleansing of the
leper; the command of Jesus to go show himself to the priest;
the leper's uncontainable joy that would not be restrained. In
this sequence, it is the command to show himself to the priest
that captures our notice. Why the priest?

Perhaps Mark is drawing a contrast here. The priest could
verify a miracle; he could not perform one. Mark is quietly saying
here that Jesus has a power that all the ritual in the world cannot
produce. He has the power to make the unclean clean.

Do you know the story of Joseph Damien? He was a Belgian
who went as a missionary to the South Sea Islands. At the age
of thirty-three he heard his bishop say one day that there was
no one to send to the leper island of Molokai and that they
would have to be left to their terrible fate alone and without
comfort. Joseph Damien decided he would go. When he arrived
on Molokai he found the lepers living lives not much better than
the beasts. For sixteen years he lived among them. He built them
a church; he built them better houses; he built them a water
supply; he loved them, cared for them, nursed them, and when
they died, he buried them.

Then, one day, death was near. Two priests and sisters of
charity knelt beside him. "When you are in heaven, Father," said

one of the priests, "will you, like Elijah, leave me your mantle?"

Joseph Damien smiled: "What would you do with my mantle?" he asked. Then he added slowly, "It is full of leprosy."[5]

Now that is a lovely story, but it has no gospel in it. It is a story of how the unclean took the clean to the ground and pinned him. But Mark's story has an added element. Here is one who came among the untouchables. His mantle, like Joseph Damien's, became full of leprosy—moral and spiritual leprosy—yours and mine. That leprosy took him to the ground. The Old Testament speaks of it beautifully: "He made his grave with the wicked" (Isa. 53:9).

But that is not the element I speak of. Joseph Damien did as much. It is not the grave that makes him our Saviour; it is resurrection! Another sentence in the old prophetic passage captures the new element: "With his stripes we are healed." He has power to make the unclean clean.

Whether it be leprosy of body or leprosy of heart, that is a miracle!

Notes

1. Dietrich Bonhoeffer, *Letters and Papers from Prison* (London: Fontana Books, Collins Press), p. 91.

2. Alexander Dru (ed.), *The Journals of Kierkegaard* (London: Fontana Books, Collins Press), p. 241.

3. Quoted by Harold A. Bosley, "Following Jesus Today," *Pulpit Digest,* April, 1965, pp. 21-22.

4. Spencer Free, "The Human Touch," in David L. George, *The Family Book of Best Loved Poems* (Garden City, New York: Hanover House, 1952).

5. William Barclay, *And He Had Compassion on Them* (Edinburgh: The Church of Scotland Youth Committee, 1955), pp. 46-47. Available through Outlook Publishers, 512 East Main Street, Richmond, Va.

5 Faith Meets Forgiveness
Mark 2:1-12

Were it possible to imagine that we knew nothing about Jesus—nothing at all—and there passed into our hands for the very first time this writing we call the Gospel of Mark, we would doubtless conclude that the author wrote from a particular bias, that he wrote to make a case. This would be apparent in the very first sentence—"Here begins the good news (gospel) of Jesus Christ the Son of God." Continuing with a quote from Isaiah, Mark proceeds at a breathless pace to string together the selected incidents from the life and ministry of the person whom he claims is Son of God.

Now it occurs to us right off that this unusual claim could be controversial: the claim that Jesus is the Son of God. No less the man himself. Nor does Mark quiet this thought; rather, he confirms it. Right off he tells of an uproar in the sabbath-day service at Capernaum; the wildfire news of Jesus' miracles; the growing hostility of the scribes, some of the people, the priests. We are no farther than the beginning of chapter two when that hostility breaks out into the open. Jesus meets the opposition head-on and comes off one up.

To understand all that is involved in this miracle account, we need to etch out the general contours of Jewish theology. One of the sharpest convictions Israel held was that God alone can forgive sin. Moreover, any illness was taken as an evidence of wrongdoing, of punishment from God. In their thinking, there was an airtight logic that had no exceptions, and it was that logic which Jesus used to drive his enemies to their knees. Here was the logic: First, all illness comes in consequence of sin; second, only God can forgive sin; therefore, power to heal means power to forgive sin. The first corollary of that proposition would be that anyone who could heal must have God's power in him.

Remembering Mark's opening sentence, we need no wild guesses to explain why this story comes right here. The point of the miracle is that Jesus can do what only God does: forgive sins. When Jesus broke the grip of paralysis he broke the grip of sin in the paralytic's life.

When we think of paralysis we think of the crippling effects that sin works in the lives of people and in society at large. Sometimes it is charged that ministers live sheltered lives; that they are out of touch with the realities; that they cannot really know what life is like. This is offered as explanation for their stance on certain social and moral questions when they arise.

But those who make such a charge have never lived in a pastor's home, nor have they followed a minister through the routine of a single day. It is precisely because he does know the seamy side of life, and the elements that contribute to it, that he resists the creeping erosion of public morals. He knows that—like the fabled camel of the desert—once the nose is under the tent it will not be long until the camel is in the tent, whole and entire. In an area of public morals a few years ago, we were told in our city that legal control was the answer. "Give us legal control," officials promised, "and we will have no more bootlegging, less drunk driving, and more respect for the law." That was the nose under the tent. Now, we are being accused of making hypocrites of those who drink; of denying them their constitutional rights; of contributing to lawlessness. Why? Because it is illegal to sell liquor by the drink in the eating establishments, casinos, and private clubs. This is the camel, and he is trying to get all of himself into the tent. There is a possibility he may succeed.

But ministers know what alcoholic beverage—legal or illegal—does. Alcohol in any form drags decent men and women down into the dark, chaotic abyss of an alcohol-hazed existence. Alcohol breaks down respect and love which is the mortar that holds a marriage together. Alcohol worms its way into the financial structure of community life and gets a death grip on any public figure that threatens its privileged parasitism. Alcohol—legal or illegal—breeds crime and lawlessness; it tarnishes and corrodes life, whether it be a person, a home, or a nation.

Ministers see firsthand the paralysis imposed by this dark, sinister force. They see the paralysis which comes from every thrust of evil. And this miracle offers hope.

Jesus is faced with paralysis—the paralysis of a man. Step by step, Mark carries us through the miracle. Faith meets forgiveness, and out of it emerges hope for any person under the mesmerizing paralysis of sin.

The three distinct thrusts in the story can be caught in three phrases: First, "four men were carrying him"; second, "when they had broken through"; third, "when Jesus saw their faith." In these thrusts is the unfolding miracle.

Bearing Others' Burdens

The story begins with someone who had to be carried. Now this is not unfamiliar; most of us know about that. Congregations, through their organizations and their ministry, carry casualties who have been struck down by one sinister force or another. One pastor ticked off some of the load he and his congregation were carrying:

The home of a successful doctor, wrecked because of infidelity. A wife who has had to leave a normal home life for an institution. A father whose uncontrolled anger and domination have antagonized his children, filling them with resentment. A schoolteacher whose anxiety and daily worry make her a marginal functioner in her work. Another woman, who by her gossip and censure of other people, constantly festers the health of her church and her community.[1]

Parents know what it is to carry. They carry their children—in provision for food, clothing, and shelter; in secular, religious, and artistic education; in emotional security and understanding.

"One of the things most lacking in our families today," says Dr. J. Louise Despert, author of *Children of Divorce,* "is the exchange of really deep, warm feeling between parents and children. Parents should realize that emotional coldness is a psychological defense."

Some warmhearted, compassionate Christians, like the four friends of the paralyzed man in the miracle story, know what it is to carry somebody else. When the apostle Paul wrote to the rough-and-ready converts in the Roman province of Galatia, he put in capsule form the gist of Christianity as it relates to others: "Bear ye one another's burdens, and so fulfil the law of Christ" (6:2).

The giving program of the church is involved in this. The whole concept of a stewardship program centers in the impulse every Christian feels to reach out to help. Some can do more to help than others, but all need to have a part.

Ruth C. Ikerman tells of a cross-country trip where the national highway offered a choice between the mountains and the valley. Here was a little wayside church. She and her husband seated themselves by a white-haired man with kindly blue eyes matching a well-worn blue tie. His coat was gray; his trousers brown. There was a scorched spot on one knee. They had no sooner taken their seats than he handed them a hymnbook.

The old man took out a blue-lined piece of tablet paper, carefully folded it, and placed it on the offering plate when it was passed. Just then an early summer breeze freshened, and catching the paper, blew it out where it floated down to the floor in front of Mrs. Ikerman. As she retrieved it, she could not help but see what was carefully written thereon: "I promise to pray."

All through the service, Mrs. Ikerman confessed, her mind kept going back to that note. She wondered what kind of story lay behind it. Finally the benediction was pronounced; the service dismissed. They fell into conversation with the old man. They found out he had a daughter in the state they called home. "I live with another daughter now," he explained, "since my wife died." They complimented him on having some family who wanted him. Finally, the conversation died and they turned to go. But he stopped them.

"About that note this morning—the folks here know how it is. Bessie—she was my wife—came down with cancer. (His blue eyes mellowed.) That took all the money there was—the house, too. My daughter gives me a home and food, and I have all the clothes I need, left over from before. Seems I'm too old to work for cash money, but a body can't let the plate go by. So each week I promise to pray for the pastor and the church. Every morning I give a full hour of prayer. Then I start on the chores at my daughter's house. Just wanted you to know how it was."[2]

Every true Christian knows how it is. It is an impulse very much like Christ—this impulse to be a part of bearing another's burdens. And this is the beginning of this particular miracle: four friends carrying a friend. That is always how a miracle starts.

> There is a destiny that makes us brothers
> None goes his way alone;
> All we send into the lives of others
> Comes back again into our own.[3]

Overcoming Obstacles

Always there are obstacles to overcome. They are here in the story, caught up in the phrase, "When they had broken through." Naturally we would think that the only obstacle was the difficulty involved in getting this man before Jesus. But there were others.

The first thing they had to break through was the sense of rejection, worthlessness—even self-pity—that had shackled this crippled man. In Palestine, in the time of Jesus, the Jews con-nected sin and suffering intimately. The rabbis had a saying: "There is no sick man healed of his sickness until all his sins have been forgiven him." To the Jews a sick man was a man with whom God was angry. When a man became ill, it was a sign God had rejected him.

The feeling of rejection is never a light burden to carry. But many carry it. Wives carry it because they never hear a word of appreciation or affection. Husbands carry it because they are not encouraged at home or at work. Teachers and church workers carry it for lack of support and reinforcement. The ill find rejection a part of their burden as they seek to understand why they were singled out. Jesus himself knew the burden of rejection. Remember the cry: "Why hast thou forsaken me?"

These friends first broke through the isolation of rejection that they might help.

A second breakthrough was the crowd. The crowd around Jesus almost kept this paralyzed man from getting close enough for a miracle.

You will recall the resourcefulness of these friends. They mounted the flat roof by the usual outside stair. Then they broke through the marled surface, removing the brush and clay that filled in between the beams, lowering their man by ropes to the feet of Jesus.

It is interesting that it was the crowd around Jesus, pressing in, that made it so very difficult to get the cripple to the place where the miracle could transpire. Sometimes, shame to say, the biggest hindrance we have in our witnessing is the crowd—members of the congregation.

Do you remember Nietzsche, the German philosopher, who has been called the spiritual father of Nazism? Did you know that Nietzsche nearly became a Christian once? When the decision was in the balance, he went to live among Christian people reputed to be very devout—just to see what Christians were like! The experiment failed, alas! He said, "These Christians will have to look a lot more redeemed before I can believe in it."[4]

One cannot help but wonder if those who pressed and thronged in upon Jesus did not themselves know someone they could have carried to him. There is no particular virtue in being in the Christian crowd; the virtue is in being a Christian.

Paul once wrote a line that sounds quite conceited: "Those things, which ye have both learned, and received, and heard, and seen in me, do" (Phil. 4:9). But this is not conceit; it is confidence. It is a confidence that arises out of the fact that he was carrying a grand host of people to Jesus—in Galatia, in Philippi, in Colossae, in Ephesus, in Corinth, in Caesarea, in Berea, in Rome, in Cyprus, on Crete. Paul had literally forgotten himself, for to him "to live was Christ."

We are probably the most Christlike when we are overcoming obstacles that stand between our friends and our Saviour.

Faith Meets Forgiveness

The final thrust of the story begins with the phrase, "When Jesus saw their faith."

Miracles do not just happen. Somebody works for them, prays for them, plans for them. Andrew Murray, the great Scottish preacher once wrote, "God works only in response to the prayer of his people." Frank Laubach was asked, "If God answers prayer, why doesn't he respond to the prayers of sincere people who pray for peace?" The veteran missionary answered, "Because the prayers are only a trickle when they must be a flood."

But prayer and work is not all of it. These are the expressions of faith. These are the outward thrust of the spirit of man for a deliverance he can never bring off by himself. In answer there is given forgiveness. And forgiveness comes only from God.

Mark took no pains to hide the fact that he was writing from a particular point of view. For him, there was no doubt: Jesus of Nazareth was the Son of God. More than that, Jesus was God, veiled in human flesh. In adoration and wonder he builds toward this miracle of the paralyzed-man-made-whole to express the faith of his own heart.

Toscanini, the world-famous conductor, was very exacting and almost tyrannical in rehearsals. Once he rehearsed an orchestra in Beethoven's *Ninth Symphony* in preparation for a concert. At last the rehearsals were over, and master and orchestra were ready for the performance. It was given. When the plaudits died away, and the curtain was drawn for the last time, the orchestra and the concert master were alone. The first violinist leaned over to the second and said, "If he scolds us after this I will jump up and push him off the platform." But Toscanini was silent, his arms outstretched, his deep eyes burning with an inner fire. After a long silence he spoke up. "Who am I? Who is Toscanini? Who are you? I am nobody. You are nobody."

The orchestra was hushed. The master still stood with arms extended. They waited in awed silence. Then, with the light of heaven on his face, he exclaimed: "Beethoven is everything— everything!"

That is what Mark is saying in this miracle where faith meets forgiveness. And everyone of us who has known forgiveness knows that Mark is right. Christ is everything!

Notes

1. Thomas S. Kepler, *Design for Living* (Nashville: Abingdon Press, 1955).

2. Ruth C. Ikerman, "The Widower's Mite." Source unknown.

3. Edwin Markham, "A Creed," *Masterpieces of Religious Verse*, ed. James Dalton Morrison (New York: Harper & Brothers, 1948), p. 464.

4. W. E. Sangster, *Can I Know God?* (Nashville: Abingdon Press, 1960), pp. 174-75.

6 What Counts with You?
Mark 3:1-6

Have you ever been thrust up against a situation where you knew you had the next move; that you could get the prize, and nobody could top you? And then, you could not quite bring yourself to make the play, for between you and the prize was somebody else who was going to get hurt, and that somebody else was as innocent as the dawn?

A minister had quietly nurtured the hope of serving his denomination some day as a member of its Foreign Mission Board. It was a place of service in which he had a vital interest. It would put him in touch with the pulse of the entire denomination as it pumped its strength into pipelines that stretched across the world. And then, it was an honor that came to very few.

One day, without ever having made a move to bring it to pass, this minister had in his hand the opportunity to make that hope come true. But to do so, he would have to clash head-on with the open interests of another minister. That would not be difficult, except for one thing: the rival minister had sent an underling to capture this position for him. Now the first minister knew the place was his for the taking; there was no question. But he also knew that to take that place would mean that the underling would go home empty-handed; that he would suffer reprisals. It was a neat little problem in human relations.

The first minister was not naïve. Clearly, here was a choice he had to make. What counted most? A denominational post or a brother who was in the unfortunate position of being caught in the squeeze? Was it the post or this person?

Well, the minister made his choice. He forfeited his dream; it is still just a dream. He chose his brother.

Now life is like that. We are on familiar ground here. In one way or another, life is shoving at us these neat little dilemmas that require a choice. In the language of chess, we must decide:

will we lose this knight and this bishop and save the queen? Or will we sacrifice the queen and win the game?

The question always boils down to this: What counts with me?

If we could remove the past tense from this brief story, it would dawn on us that Mark has captured here in concentrated form one of those neat little life-situations. Each of those involved in the story is unconsciously deciding what counts most for him. But more than that, we find ourselves involved, too. For we identify with one of the principals. Each is asking, what counts with me? The Pharisees ask the question; Jesus asks it; the afflicted stonemason asks it.

The Pharisees

It is significant beyond mere curiosity that the Jews had taken the sabbath and thoroughly skewed it. Not that it was intentional; not that. Rather, it was that in their intense preoccupation with what God had said they did not hear what God was saying. The Jews took seriously the Word of God. For example, they had taken the Ten Commandments and developed eight hundred pages of commentary on them. Sixty-four and a half columns—better than thirty-two pages—were devoted to the law of the sabbath.[1] They were trying to make clear what the Word of God said.

But in their preoccupation with the fine print, they lost the spirit of the sabbath completely. One of the categories of work (forbidden, of course, on the sabbath) was healing. Steps could be taken to keep a man from getting worse but not to make him any better.

Now that may be silly to us. To the Pharisees, it was as serious as heaven and hell. They were a little like the Billy Rankin Jack Wilkins tells about in the *National Observer*. In 1899, Billy Rankin was a schoolteacher who went out to the Snake River territory in Idaho to do a little prospecting. One day a couple of surveyors and a geologist came along, charting a course for a railroad. The geologist told Billy that from all indications the hill was near solid copper in the center. And that sent Billy off. He started digging a hole in that hill to get to the center. Every couple of years he would go out and work in a sawmill for enough dynamite to come back and blast deeper into his hole. He dug in that hole for fifty years, until he died. One of the men around there remarked about Billy when he died, "He threw his whole life into that hole."[2] That could be said of the Pharisees and their traditions.

The Pharisees had a very natural instinct to protect what was important to them. In Jesus they sensed a threat. He did not have a proper sense of reverence for that "hole" into which they had thrown their collective lives.

The Pharisees' security was in a system—a rigid structure. This is why we resist change; why we close our minds to new truth; why we refuse to admit a new way of looking at things; why we become vaguely hostile before a different structuring of things.

The Pharisees decided that the thing that counted most with them was this "hole" they had been digging in all these generations. Their rigid theology just could not bend to make room for Jesus.

Jesus

Jesus had to face the question, What counts with me?

The grim-faced Pharisees and scribes were eloquent in their silence. Were I to make a defense plea for them it would be that they were contending for the right—as they saw it. The very name "Pharisee" means separated one. They made it the one business of their lives to so live that they never broke any of the eight hundred pages of regulations implicit in the Commandments. The Pharisees may have been a sorry lot; they were also a dead serious lot.

We may be sure that Jesus had a very clear idea of what crossing these people could mean. There were so many other little exits he could have taken. For example, he could have stayed away from the synagogue and avoided the situation altogether. He could have excused himself from the congregation on grounds of an urgent appointment. He could have waited until the sabbath was over. He could have ignored the man who was less than whole.

But even to mention these all-too-familiar ruses we employ is to blush. Somehow they do not seem to fit in the same breath with the name Jesus. And it makes us blush, too, when we admit that what is so inadmissible with Jesus is so admissible with us.

There is the story about a man who asked the artist Whistler to come to his home and tell him what was wrong about the hanging of a picture. He said that no way or place he hung it seemed to be quite right. Whistler went, looked the situation over, and then announced, "Sir, the trouble is that you are trying to make the picture fit the room; you must make the room fit the picture."[3]

Too often we want to alter the picture instead of our lives.

But if the grim-faced Pharisees presented one aspect of this tight little life-situation, the perversion of truth presented the other. For what Jesus knew in his heart was that somewhere in the limbo of tradition the truth had been lost. The first sabbath, when it was given, was given to man. The stars knew no sabbath; they continued whirling in their orbits. The sun and the moon did not interrupt their appointed race. The buds, the bees, the birds, the animals, the fish—they all continued their animated bustling activity of life. Man and his Creator—only these two—knew anything at all about a sabbath.

The sabbath stood as a symbol, as a link between man and his Maker. This one thing they, and they alone, kept together. The sabbath was made for man, to remind him that his destiny was far above the earth and earthy things. It was made that his mind might contemplate the far horizons, that his heart might beat with the heart of the eternal Father.

What had man done with the sabbath? He had erected this vast, impossible hodgepodge, the end effect of which was to make a religious man rigidly self-righteous and introspective while scandalously insensitive to the most obvious concerns of a brother. It denied the very thing the Heavenly Father had designed it to do: make men into a loving family. Jesus knew what he had to do.

It is pretty clear to us, too, from this distance. But what of those conflicts that lie closer? Tradition has a tendency to drift from the truth that sired it. Institutions have a way of developing an instinct for survival. Vested interests make the shiniest truth opaque.

Perhaps that stubborn New England noncomformist Ralph Waldo Emerson overstated his case, but there is some truth in what he said about this: "God offers to every mind its choice between the truth and repose. Take which you please—you can never have both. . . . He in whom the love of repose dominates . . . gets rest, commodity, and reputation; but he shuts the door to truth."

If we took a real hard look at our own lives, our homes, our congregational life—these things so close to us—we might be driven to conclude that we have in this little story a conflict that is more than ancient history.

Like our Saviour, we may find it necessary to choose between a well-intentioned but misdirected pattern and an obvious human need.

The Stonemason

The third principal of the story is the man with the withered hand. There is an old gospel not included in our New Testament called *The Gospel to the Hebrews*. Most of it is lost, but we have enough to know it existed. It is this gospel which the great fifth-century scholar Jerome quotes in his writing about Matthew's account of this miracle: "I was a stonemason seeking to earn my living with my hands: I pray you, Jesus, give me back my health that I may not have to beg my bread in shame."[4] This quote is behind the tradition that the man in question was a stonemason.

We need not reflect long on this appeal before it sinks in that there is in the appeal a decision. He is resolved to run whatever risk, to accept whatever uncertainty, to embrace whatever unknown, that he might identify with Jesus.

The old system might be a security for the scribes and the Pharisees; it was a prison for him. The illusions of the synagogue might be enough for some; the stonemason needed truth. In Jesus he sensed he had found what he needed.

The reward of his faith is known to us all, a part of it at least. We know that he was made whole. But is that all? We must not forget that Mark, who recorded the story first, is writing for a verdict—my verdict and yours. And here is just one more witness —a man who had to decide what counted most with him: the relative comfort and security of a half-life or the possibility of a whole life, which could be had only through risk and possible pain. He made the choice; he took the risk; he won the prize. He was made a whole man, in body and in soul.

There are some who insist on a life that is something less than whole. A husband who insists on drinking, even though he knows it is an albatross around his neck. A wife who continues her inane hypochondria, when she knows that her wretched self-preoccupations are wrecking her family. A teen-ager who keeps on with his silly pattern of infantile rebellion, even when he knows that he hurts himself more than any other. And all of us—sinners that we are—clinging to crumpled little vestiges of security, like a child to its blanket, rather than casting them off, with an appeal for help filled with high resolve.

Amos Wells has a moving poem in which he captures the full dimension of the miracle:

> Praise God! Praise God! Give me my tools again!
> Oh! Let me grasp a hammer and a saw!
> Bring me a nail, and any piece of wood,
> Come, see me shut my hand and open it,
> And watch my nimble fingers twirl a ring.
> How good are solids!—oak, and stone, and iron,
> And rough and smooth and straight and curved and round!
> Here, Rachel: for these long and weary years
> My hand has ached to smooth your shining hair
> And to touch your dimpled cheek. Come wife and see
> *I am a man again,* a man for work,
> A man for earning bread and clothes and home.
> A man, no more a bandaged cumberer.
> And did you hear them muttering at Him?
> And did you see them looking sour at me?
> They'll cast me from the synagogue, perchance:
> But let them: I've a hand, a hand, a hand!
> And, ah, dear wife, to think He goes about
> So quietly, and does such things as this,
> *Making poor half men whole.*[5]

Mark tells us this story to tell us that the thing which should count most with us is the fact that Jesus can do a wonderful thing like this for you and for me.

Notes

1. Barclay, *And He Had Compassion on Them, op. cit.,* p. 98.

2. *National Observer,* November 23, 1924.

3. H. I. Hester and J. Winston Pearce, *Broadman Comments 1963* (Nashville: Broadman Press), p. 408.

4. Quoted in Barclay, *And He Had Compassion on Them,* p. 103.

5. In *ibid.,* pp. 106-7.

7 The Storm and the Saviour
Mark 4:35-41

There are differences in the miracles of Jesus. Most of them have to do with persons: a leper, a blind man, a woman with a terrible hemorrhage, a desperately sick child or servant. But there are others with a completely different thrust. They are nature miracles: unusually bold exploits involving the very elements.

Interpreters have had different approaches to this special kind of miracle. Some have ignored the fact that the miracle involves control of the elements; they have focused on the persons. Ronald Wallace finds four truths in this Scripture passage: fear overcoming faith; faith overcoming fear; the Word that creates faith and controls fear; and the majesty and lowliness of him who speaks.[1]

In contrast is a passage in Alan Richardson's book on the miracle stories of the Gospels. He sees the story as an affirmation of faith by the infant church in the lordship of Christ; a lordship that extends over nature and history. Recalling that the Gospel of Mark emerges out of the days of Nero's persecution, he says: "It might seem to the faint-hearted that the Lord was asleep and indifferent to their peril; but in truth He is present in the Church, and will arise and cast out the demon of the storm. . . . (It) is a message of comfort to a storm-tossed Church in a hostile world."[2]

Doubtless both approaches are true. In the story it is quite clear that there is a witness to our own need to have faith. But soaring over and undergirding that truth is the magnificent witness that we do not face life's storms unaided; that there is one with us in life who "has the whole world in his hand"; that we have more hope than could be afforded by our own grit, nerve, and savvy. Lying quietly here in this lovely little story is the mighty assertion that Jesus of Galilee is the Lord of life, of man, and of man's world.

Three impressions come through the storyteller's art. First, the storm; next, the calm; finally, the Saviour.

The Storm

"A heavy squall came on and the waves broke over the boat until it was all but swamped" (Mark 4:37, NEB).[3] Could there be any clearer picture of the human predicament than this?

We look at the intact world about us, and this picture seems faithful to that which we see. Men and women drowning in a sea of alcohol is too much a part of our culture. A cold war turning hot in isolated spots threatens to burst into a holocaust that will destroy us all. Homes falling apart; teen-agers dramatizing the grotesque world they live in by their jerky, preoccupied, exhibitionist dress and dance; middle-agers muddling through frenzied, frenetic days on a combination of black coffee and tranquilizers. The storm is dark enough that many of the old landmarks have disappeared. The world around us finds itself in the picture of the storm.

But there is more. Sometime during adolescence we wake up to the grim fact that we have a death sentence hanging over our own heads and the ground under our feet is about as firm as quicksand. And it does not get any better as we get older; it gets worse.

In the preparation of this material the telephone rang. It was a death call. Immediately I went to the home of one of our members to comfort a son in the death of his mother. Nine years before I had been on a similar mission because of the death of his father. While he was attending some detail about the funeral, his wife told me of a recent grief that had come to her sister: an only son, thirty-six years of age, had been killed in an automobile accident in Texas, leaving behind his widow and five children.

In reply, I recounted Tolstoy's fable in which a traveler is pursued by a wild beast. In an effort to save himself, he gets into a waterless well, but at the bottom of it he sees a dragon with its jaws wide open, ready to devour him. He dares not get out for fear of the wild beast and dares not descend for fear of the dragon, so he catches hold of the branch of a wild plant growing in a crevice of the wall. His arms grow tired, but still he holds on. Then he sees two mice, one black and one white, gradually nibbling their way around the stem of the wild plant on which he is hanging. Soon the plant will give way and he will fall into the jaws of the dragon. The traveler knows he must inevitably perish. Then (with a characteristic Russian touch of irony) he notices a few drops of honey on a leaf of the wild plant, and he reaches out to lick them for strength to hold on.

"Now," I continued, "that is a picture of life if this existence is all of it. Such events as the Texas accident mock us unless we have a hope that looks beyond the intact world we know so well. Within the framework of life as we experience it, and without the Christian hope, we can only conclude with Shakespeare, 'Life is a tale, told by an idiot, full of sound and fury, signifying nothing.' Life without the Christian hope adds up to a cipher."

I was merely putting into words her own feelings at that moment. Haven't we all had such moments?

The first impression of the Scripture story is this wild, lashing, senseless storm that breaks over the boat and the men, threatening to destroy them all.

The Calm

The second impression comes with this fragment of a sentence: "He was in the stern, asleep on a cushion." The contrast is further drawn by the next events: "They roused him and said, 'Master, we are sinking! Do you not care?' He stood up, rebuked the wind, and said to the sea, 'Hush! Be still!' The wind dropped and there was a dead calm" (vv. 39-40, NEB).

Could it be that Mark is assuring us here that when we take seriously the presence of Jesus in the storm that then the storm becomes a calm?

What storm are you passing through?

Is it sorrow? Think again about Tolstoy's fable. But this time add the fact that Jesus, the Son of God, has hung from that same tenuous root; that he did the dragon in; that he clambered back out of that pit only to see that the beast had slunk away. (It turned out the beast and the dragon were in cahoots.) See him now as he comes over to the edge of your own private little pit, extending a hand downward, saying, "Here, take my hand! Trust me! I will deliver you."

Such reflection makes the storm of sorrow a calm.

Or is it some situation-problem? As you projected the next

few months or years, you thought you had everything worked out. You were on top of the situation. Then, out of nowhere, came this sudden turn of events. Suddenly the whole thing was cast in a new light altogether—a bad light, you would say.

To further complicate matters, you—as a serious Christian— had become convinced that the plan you had worked out was God's will. Now what?

Perhaps the clue we search for can be found in the life of Jesus. Near the end, Jesus seemed to be a little confused; he was not sure he knew the master plan. He could see what was coming, but (quite naturally) he did not like it, and prayed, "Lord—if it be possible—let this cup pass from me." Yet, he faced that tough situation as it developed, right on through to the cross and the tomb. That was the ultimate, the final boundary situation. That was the very worst life could throw at him. And in it, Jesus was sustained; yes, vindicated.

When we reflect on our Lord's suffering, it dawns on us that this vindication was after the event. In Gethsemane it was different. There he was by no means sure. What else does the bloody sweat mean if not genuine anguish? And anguish about what appeared to be God's will? Oh, Jesus could have kicked out at any point—run up the white flag and all would have been over. He would have come out intact, except for his integrity; except for loyalty to truth; except for the will of God, as it shaped up in that given situation. And the choice was real; it involved genuine pain either way.

So you are caught in the eye of some problem situation. How calm the storm? Take that situation as "the thing given" and start from there. Within "the thing given," do the very best you know how to do, be faithful to the truth, and leave the rest in the hands of the Father.

That is what Jesus did. Later, he saw the travail of his soul and was satisfied. Jesus is our Saviour and is therefore different from us. Everything that is true of him is not necessarily true of us, but this one thing we have in common: our trust is that in the storms of life we can trust the Father. Mistrust is unworthy of him and of us. This thought will calm any storm.

Or, is yours a storm of passion? You start out the new day determined to make it a better day. But before many hours pass, you lose your temper and say things better left unsaid; or your resolution melts, and you sink back into old habits you had resolved to break. You find yourself in a dither, thoughts chasing around in your mind until the whole thing is a blur. And with things out of focus, you sink into something less than your best self.

Barclay tells of a French courtier who had a very ungovernable temper. He was always breaking out and doing and saying things for which he was sorry afterwards. A friend knew just the kind of thing which annoyed him. One day, when this courtier was actually in the king's presence at court, one of these annoying events happened. The courtier kept his temper. Later his friend said to him: "I was watching you the other day at court, and when that thing happened, I was surprised to see how well you kept your temper."

The courtier answered, "I had to keep my temper. The king was there, and I couldn't lose my temper in front of him."

His friend looked at him and said quietly: "I wish that you would try to remember that, wherever you are, you are in the presence of the King of kings."[4]

Such a thought will calm the storm of passion.

The Saviour

"Who can this be whom even the wind and the sea obey?" (cf. v. 41).

Before we answer that question we must consider the scene in that boat at sea. To these hard-bitten fishermen who knew the sea like the palm of their hand, Jesus was their responsibility. They were the weather-beaten veterans who had the courage and the sea legs. In the beginning Peter, James, and the rest felt quite equal to the task of navigating the eight miles across the sea.

A storm changed all that. Condescension oozed out with their rising fear. When they turned to Jesus, it was a desperation measure, and they could never forget what happened. Peter—even as an old man—could never tell the story without radiating again sheer wonder at just who it was who rode in that boat that day with him. For this was the Lord, not only of man, but of man's world! This is the unframed answer to the question with which the story closes.

Today, if we will admit it, our little boat is not much different. We thought we were adequate skippers—we really believed it. But the storm has descended and our little ship—in spite of all the built-in shock absorbers—is about to swamp. Our boats are preposterous sieves, and we know it.

This miracle story with its quaint little question tacked on at the end has a thrust that runs far deeper than we would guess at the first. Perhaps we can frame that thrust with our own tentative question: "Would not the one who first made our world and us, the one who first put us together, would he not be the one who could save us?"

This is a nature miracle, one of the few in the New Testament. The nature miracles are different from the others in that they assert the lordship of Christ, not only over the individual man, but over his world. The nature miracles see Christ as God, "who has the whole world in his hand." Whatever God is, Christ is.

Nothing less than this exalted view of Christ would make Jesus a Saviour. Only when we see him as the one who holds the oceans as a pool in his palm can we cast ourselves upon him in the storm and find a perfect calm in our hearts. Mark, who faithfully reflects in his Gospel the experiences and faith of Peter—whom he first heard tell these stories—is bearing his witness that Jesus is (in the fullest sense) the Saviour, even as the first Christmas angels sang upon the mountain. But more than that, this wonderful Saviour is in our little boat with us. He will never leave us nor forsake us. He will remain with us through the final hour.

Henry J. Taylor, famous American journalist, writes of an early boyhood experience that he never forgot. His father was a mine owner. A new elevator was being installed, and before the proper cage was fitted, a descent had to be made in a barrel at the end of a rope. Taylor went down in the barrel with his father. It was a terrifying experience, with the barrel swaying at the end of the rope, knocking against the sides of the shaft. Young Henry's heart was beating like a trip-hammer; he was terrified. But his father's strong arm was around him and his father's voice kept saying, "Don't be afraid, Son." When they got to the foot of the shaft, they emerged into a strange, dark, and frightening underground world. A miner came up and warned them to be careful of gas, and the warning made bad things worse. The only sure thing in that whole terrifying situation was Henry Taylor's father. A miner came up to the boy and said, "Aren't you scared?"

"Well," answered the boy honestly, "I'd be awfully scared except my father is with me."[5]

Mark's world was a dangerous one, as is ours. This Scripture story is both a confession and an affirmation. He is saying, in effect, "I would be awfully scared except that the Saviour is with me." Honesty compels us to admit that it is no different with us.

Notes

1. Ronald S. Wallace, *The Gospel Miracles* (Grand Rapids, Michigan: Eerdman's, 1963), pp. 57-63.

2. Alan Richardson, *The Miracle-Stories of the Gospel* (London: SCM Press Ltd., 56 Bloomsbury St., republished 1963), p. 92.

3. The Delegates of the Oxford University Press and the Syndics of the Cambridge University Press 1961.

4. Barclay, *And He Had Compassion on Them,* p. 95.

5. Quoted in *ibid.,* p. 96.

8 The Taming of Legion
Mark 5:1-17

Our Scripture story must have been the teacher of such consummate storytellers as Dickens or Stevenson—particularly the tack of opening the story with a sense of dread. Even in this condensed version we find a strong element of suspense.

The distinguished preacher Leslie Weatherhead, drawing on his own moods and sensations while on a visit to the actual site of this miracle story, fills in some of the details:

On a blazing June morning in 1934, I found this place strangely uncanny, weirdly desolate. If it made that impression on a Western mind on a sunny June morning, after a peaceful voyage in a motor boat, we can imagine the effect produced on the minds of the superstitious disciples, who thought pigs were unclean and graveyards full of devils, in the dusk of the late evening as they landed on what to them was a foreign shore, after a terrifying voyage during which they had been almost drowned.[1]

In the first two verses of our story, Mark scores an unusual and dramatic flair. He is convinced that Jesus has the power to tame the wild impulses, the unharnessed powers, the unbridled forces that threaten to stampede every life at one time or another. Which of us has not known some secret dread, some unadmitted weakness, some latent fissure that threatened to break loose and destroy all the work of the years? James Reston has written a book entitled *Ride the Wild Horses*. It is the same idea.

So the story begins in a mood of suspense and concludes with the suspense resolved. The wild, broken caricature of a man is restored and functioning. Between the opening suspense and the closing denouement is this unique story of the taming of Legion.

The story has three parts: the taming of Legion; the indifferent community; and the new man in the old setting.

The Taming of Legion

The sudden appearance of this panting psychopath must have scared the disciples half out of their wits. Each of the Synoptic Gospels gives us a graphic description of this weird, eerie character, accosting them in the half-light of late twilight, naked and wild-eyed, broken chains dangling from wrists and ankles, wallowing at the feet of Jesus, wailing to be left alone (v. 7).

Today modern psychology and psychiatry have coined a lot of new names like paranoia, schizophrenia, manic-depressive, and the like. The talk is about mental illness and nervous breakdowns. But in New Testament times they said that if a man got far enough removed from reality he was demon-possessed.

Both today and then the language has reference to the same thing: the power of evil to destroy a life's usefulness and meaning.

Is it not significant that this man lived in a graveyard? All his hopes, all his dreams, all his aspirations were dead. He went on living physically, but the higher instincts were dampened out— or so it would seem.

The New Testament tells us that men and women who do not have Christ in their hearts are "dead in their trespasses and sins." What can this mean except that in a deathlike sleep lie the instincts for prayer, for fellowship with the Heavenly Father, for sharing the pain of others, and for worship? Legion was in the iron grip of darkness, and all the higher centers of his being were shut up to silence and darkness, too.

When we reflect on this poor man Legion, and recognize in him some of our own tendencies toward personality disorganization, we begin to see the point of this whole story. Legion was the end result of what the power of evil can do to any of us. Evil does not exist by itself; it exists where it can feed on something good. Legion was possessed; he had been taken over by disintegrating forces. Is there any hope for Legion, or for any others like him?

The disciples certainly were asking themselves that question as Legion lay wallowing in the dirt, crying like a banshee.

Sometimes we ask that question, but not about Legion. It is about a son, a daughter, a husband, a friend, a kinsman, ourselves. Can this terrible process of self-loathing and self-destruction be reversed? Can this young man control his appetite for drink? This young woman her crippling self-doubts? At a certain point, the human spirit seems to turn on itself, like a fox gnawing at her paw caught in the trap. Dostoevski, the Russian novelist, has a paragraph in his "Notes from the Underground," which has elements of the common human experience we all recognize:

I got to the point of feeling a sort of secret abnormal despicable enjoyment in returning home to my corner on some disgusting Petersburg night, acutely conscious that that day I had committed a loathsome action again, that what was done could never be undone, and secretly, inwardly gnawing at myself for it, tearing and consuming myself till at last the bitterness turned into a sort of shameful accursed sweetness, and at last—into positive, real enjoyment! . . . The enjoyment was just from the too intense consciousness of one's own degradation; it was from feeling oneself that one had reached the last barrier, that it was horrible but that it could not be otherwise; that there was no escape for you; that you never could become a different man; that even if time and faith were still left to you to change into something different you would most likely not wish to change; or if you did wish to, even then you would do nothing; because perhaps in reality there was nothing for you to change into.[2]

The witness of Mark is that for Legion—either the one in the story or the one you know—there is a hope. A careful reading of the story suggests the possibility that the demoniac of Gadara was a particularly stubborn case. At first, Jesus merely admonished the man and his unclean spirits, but there was no real deliverance (v. 8).

And so Jesus, with patience undaunted, takes a new tack: "What is your name?" he asks. Now never had this man put in so many words just what his need was. Never had he faced his moment of truth. Never had he dared to admit he was the problem; that he must change into something better. But now all this came in upon him at once: What is your name?

There is no help for any man or woman caught in the toils of a depraved will and a sullied life until that man or woman will admit the need that exists. The alcoholic must admit his need for alcohol. The sensualist must admit his need of the sensual. The fearful must admit his need of fear. The gossiper must admit his need to gossip.

We understand all this. Does Legion?

Slowly, he frames the words on which his redemption hangs: "My name is Legion: for we are many."

This admission does not come easy for any of us. We pride ourselves on our self-reliance, our ability to make it on our own.

Then Jesus comes to us through the preaching of the Word—in such a moment as this—and with infinite kindness he speaks to us the truth of our terrible weakness. It is not easy to take. It disturbs us. But it is the only way to break the grip of evil.

The swine, plunging pell-mell into the sea, is dramatic evidence that Legion is delivered. The fragments have been fused. The loose ends that have been flailing his life out are now bound in Jesus Christ. His life has a new center. Legion has been tamed.

An Indifferent Community

The second part of this miracle story reflects an all-too-familiar situation. The outcry of the citizens of Gadara over the loss of their pigs reflects the mood of indifference and plain resentment which many of us feel when approached by the church, the Red Cross, the United Givers' Fund, the Salvation Army, or a dozen other organizations which call for our help. We solve our dilemma by making token contributions—enough to ease the hurt of our own conscience, scarcely enough to genuinely help.

Perhaps we have here one of the most genuine thrusts into our own lives from this entire story: the impulse to remain aloof, to keep uninvolved. Gabriel H. Mason, in *The Hard Sayings of Jesus,* says there are five levels of response to the needs of others:

On the first level men say, "We hate you and we'll kill you." That's *extermination.* This is what Philadelphia, Mississippi, said to the three who came into their town to help register Negro voters.

On the second level we say,"We hate you, but we'll use you." That's *exploitation.* Politics thrives on this level, whether it's the politics of government, economics, or religion.

On the third level of response we say, "We don't like you, but we'll let you alone." That's *toleration.* This finds many of us.

On the fourth level, men say, "You are different from me, but I know your worth." That's *appreciation.*

One other level—the fifth and highest—is to say, "I appreciate you, and I will help you realize all your latent powers and capacities." That's *redemptive love.*

Nobody in Gadara rose above the third level, and most of us still live in Gadara. Studdert Kennedy, in his poem entitled "Indifference," tells us how a failure of genuine response hurts Christ, whether in the first century or the twentieth:

When Jesus came to Golgotha they hanged him on a tree,
They drave great nails through hands and feet, and made a Calvary;
They crowned him with a crown of thorns, red were his wounds and deep,
For those were crude and cruel days, the human flesh was cheap.

When Jesus came to Birmingham, they simply passed him by,
They never hurt a hair of him, they only let him die;
For men had grown more tender, and they would not give him pain,
They only just passed down the street, and left him in the rain.

Still Jesus cried, "Forgive them, for they know not what they do,"
And still it rained the winter rain that drenched him through and through;
The crowds went home and left the streets without a soul to see,
And Jesus crouched against a wall and cried for Calvary.[3]

One word from the New Testament, and we move on to the final part of the story. "But if any one has the world's goods and sees his brother in need, yet closes his heart against him, how does God's love abide in him? Little children, let us not love in word or speech but in deed and in truth" (1 John 3:17-18, RSV).

The New Man in the Old Setting

Legion is a new creature now, but there is still the old town, the old crowd, the old habits. He wants to go with Jesus, to get away from the old scenes, the taunting faces, the haunting memories. But flight would prove nothing; Jesus insists that he stay right there in Gadara.

Kipling has a poem called "Mulholland's Contract." Mulholland was a cattleman on a ship. Once on a voyage a violent storm descended, and between decks the cattle broke loose. Mulholland was in imminent danger of death either from their plunging hoofs or their lunging horns, and in that moment he made a contract with God:

> An' by the terms of the Contract, as I have read the same
> If He got me to port alive I would exalt His name.
> An' praise His Holy Majesty till further orders came.

Miraculously he was preserved, and Mulholland determined to keep his contract:

> An' I spoke to God of our Contract, an' He says to my prayer:
> "I never puts on my ministers no more than they can bear.
> So back you go to the cattle-boats an' preach My Gospel there."

> I didn't want to do it, for I knew what I should get;
> An' I wanted to preach religion, handsome and out of the wet;
> But the Word of the Lord were laid on me, an' I done what I was set.[4]

Legion would rather have lived out this new life in Christ "handsome and out of the wet."

It is of more than passing interest that he did not, for this story took place in the one uniquely Gentile center of all Palestine, the Decapoloi. It was a confederation of ten self-governing quasi-independent, Greek cities. Could it be that Mark uses this quiet means to remind us that the Jesus of Galilee knows no boundaries—either of race, geography, or time?

Notes

1. Quoted in David A. Redding, *The Miracles of Christ* (Westwood, N. J.: Fleming H. Revell, 1964), p. 144.

2. Thomas Mann, *The Short Novels of Dostoevski,* translation reprint copy by Dial Press, 1945, pp. 130-33. "Notes from the Underground," copyright The Macmillan Co., New York. Used by permission.

3. G. A. Studdert Kennedy, "Indifference," in *The Unutterable Beauty* (London: Hodder & Stoughton, 1964), p. 31.

4. Rudyard Kipling, "Mulholland's Contract," in *Collected Verse* (New York: Doubleday & Co., 1907), pp. 42-44.

9 You Are Important
Mark 5:21-43

Five expressions which Mary B. Compton calls "the most important words in communication" are:

I am proud of you.
What is your opinion?
If you please.
Thank you.
You.

The common denominator here is the little personal pronoun "you." To use any of these expressions is to manifest an interest in the most important person in the world—you.

One of the signs of a really genuine person is an interest in the other person. Such a person does not think in terms of crowds, or faceless mobs; he centers on the one person. He has the capacity to give—if even for a moment—all of himself to another.

Barclay tells the story of Evelyn Bell, who was a student of the violin. The famous violinist Kubelik was to give a concert in Queen's Hall in London. Her teacher gave her an introduction to Kubelik and she went to ask him for a ticket, since there were none to be had at the ticket office. Kubelik told her that he could do nothing; that there was not room for a mouse in Queen's Hall for that concert.

"What am I to do about the concert?" she asked, almost weeping. "If I can't get a ticket, I will never hear you play."

"O, but you will!" said Kubelik. "Sit there!" And Kubelik played his concert program to an audience of one.[1]

Jesus is like that. With him the supreme unit of value is the one person. People of his day seemed to sense that he was very close to the Messiah image about which Isaiah wrote (40:11; 42:3; 61:12). Never did Jesus break the bruised reed.

This was in sharp contrast with his enemies, the Pharisees and the priests. For them the most important consideration was the religious system that had been building up for the last five hundred years. The religious establishment they espoused had long since lost any sensitivity to the needs—or for that matter, the differences—of people. You either fit in or it ground you to powder, and with a magnificent indifference. Everybody knew that. And the very contrast between the religious leaders and Jesus made the common people love Jesus even more.

The art of our storyteller tends to obscure the fact that within this one story there are actually three: first, a father in conflict; second, an outcast in despair; and finally, the child in the grip of death. In each, the person is of supreme importance.

A Father in Conflict

The story opens with Jairus on his knees at the feet of Jesus, imploring him to go home with him to his sick daughter. What an opening scene, were this being staged as a play! But even more dramatic is the quiet, even desperate, internal struggle that has already been resolved in Jairus' heart. So our opening scene is the closing scene of a drama more exciting by far than this public plea.

The clue to this internal drama is given in the phrase "one of the rulers of the synagogue." In the circles in which he moved, Jairus was an important man. He had arrived at the top of the heap in the local power struggle. He was a "ruler of the synagogue." In this position he helped arrange the services; helped manage the financial affairs; decided who would make the prayers, read the Scriptures, deliver the sermon. Doubtless Jairus set his cap for this place of prestige and authority long before it came to him. The way to this lofty prominence had been long, devious, demanding. Jairus knew what he wanted; he had paid the price.

Not that it was all that cold and calculating. The ambition was salted with genuine piety. But the ambition and the drive to power were there. After all, Jairus was human—was he not?

And being human, Jairus doted on his little twelve-year-old daughter. In the galaxy of interests that whirred about his life, his daughter was probably the brightest light. When she became ill, and then later when it dawned on Jairus that he was about to lose her, his whole scheme of things fell in a jumble. There came slipping into his mind a possibility that simply tore him up: could it be possible that this Jesus would have power to help his little daughter?

To go to Jesus was to toss everything he had prized to the winds. Jairus was no Johnny-come-lately. He knew how the religious leaders felt about Jesus; he had no illusions on how they would feel about one of their own seeking out Jesus and asking for help. Which was more important, being a ruler of the synagogue or being a father?

Such were the ingredients of Jairus' struggle.

This kind of conflict is not strange to us. In one way or another most of us parents have had to face a similar question.

When the children of Israel came into Canaan from the land of Egypt, they found an abhorrent religious practice among the people there. In the language of the Bible, they "passed their children through the fire." That means that the mothers and fathers of Canaan offered their own children as sacrifices on an altar of flame.

We cringe at the very thought of such a thing. Yet, I know of mothers and fathers who do the same thing today. There is no stench of burning flesh; no anguished cries of dying children. It is more civilized than that. But the end result is the same; it just takes longer to make the sacrifice. The altars of modern parents are quite prosaic, too. It may be the thirst for a long, cool one in the late evening and the sure instinct that to hold to that and to be active in church would not go together. So they cling to the long, cool glass. Or it may be pride—pure pride.

A parent says, "What have they got up there at church that I haven't got? I'm as good as any of them!" And the truth is, he is probably right; particularly about his professed virtue. But what the proud man misses is that no one in church makes a claim to virtue. His very identification with the church is an admission of his need of a Saviour. And there are other fathers and mothers who sacrifice their children to a schedule: they give their children everything but themselves.

Perhaps it is indifference. Here is a father who has made it very well up to this point without any vital contact with the church, or with Christian faith. But now he has some children who are on the threshold of adolescence. Having been over the way himself, he knows well the hazards, the pitfalls, the risks. And deep inside him he also knows that he has not met *all* the needs of his children. The unspoken fact is that after he has provided shelter, food, clothes, and acceptance, there is another need. It is the need to worship, to have faith, to offer strength and comfort long after he is dead and gone. He feels it himself now; he knows his children will feel it one day, too. And this is the time for him to rethink his pattern, to reconstruct his scheme of values, to alter his stance.

Are you like Jairus—in conflict? I could wish that you would resolve your conflict as well and as wisely as did he when he came kneeling at the feet of Jesus!

An Outcast in Despair

The wisdom of Jairus is reflected in the next sentence of the story: "Jesus went with him" (v. 24).

They had not gone far till there was an interruption. Even the flow of the story is suspended. This is the story within the story, the miracle within the miracle. It is evidence—for the second time—of how the Saviour's heart went out to the single person.

This time it was a woman, suffering from a dual misfortune. The most obvious of her troubles was her exhausting and wearying sickness. She had no strength for anything, except the most desperate necessities.

Her sickness had generated a second misfortune more desperate than the first. She was an outcast. According to the laws of her religion (Lev. 15:25-30), she was fit for nothing. The bed she slept in, the clothes she wore, the chair she sat in, the people she touched—everything was defiled by contact with her. Worship was denied her; social concourse forbidden. This was her desperation.

The necessity that drove her was the need to break this awful cycle of circumstance; to break out of this suffocating stricture; to shed this terrible curse. So desperate was she that she was willing to break the laws of her religion, to go out into the crowd; to reach out and touch the passing Saviour.

Now this poor, worn little woman had no assurance—none at

all—that what she was daring to do would bring any relief. It might result in nothing better than further reprisals. After this venture, there was the possibility that her little world would collapse altogether.

We never know—do we—just what burden the person next to us may be bearing? Whatever Jairus may have felt about this interruption, Jesus recognized the desperation of the woman; took the time; healed her. This little nobody was important to the Saviour.

Perhaps you are one who feels as this little outcast must have felt.

Years ago, Mr. Whitmore, of the Door of Hope in New York City, wrote a book. On the title page were two faces—one, hard and bitter with deep lines; the other, an expression of sweetness, gentleness, and purity. Both belonged to the same person, at least physically. The photographs had been made one year apart.

Blue Bird, the denizen of the slums of New York, came to the Door of Hope in a degraded condition. There she heard of Jesus and learned to believe in him, to love him, and to trust him. The story behind the pictures was the story of her transformation.

Perhaps the ugliness which needs transformation in your life is not so much *morality* as *attitude; behavior* as *personality.* Plagued by feelings of inferiority, inadequacy, social clumsiness, perhaps you need to say:

> Dear Lord, take up my tangled skeins,
>   Where I have wrought in vain;
> That by the skill of Thy dear hands
>   Some beauty may remain.
>
> Touch Thou the sad, discordant keys
>   Of my poor, troubled breast,
> And change to peaceful harmonies
>   The sighings of unrest.
>
> Take all my failures, each mistake
>   Of my poor, human ways,
> Then, Saviour, for Thine own dear sake,
>   Make them show forth Thy praise.[2]

A Child in the Grip of Death

Once the interruption is worked through, Jairus and Jesus resume their journey. In essence, these events follow: a servant comes to advise Jairus that all is for nought—his daughter is dead; Jesus encourages the grief-stricken father to "have faith"; they come to the home to find the mourners (a professional function) have already taken over; Jesus dismisses them, while they heap on their scorn; with the parents and Peter, James, and John, Jesus enters the small girl's chamber, closes the door, and then restores her to the parents' loving arms.

Beyond the bare events lies this quiet question: What is the writer of this Gospel telling us?

Perhaps the clue is in the time when it was written. Many scholars think that Mark was written within the same decade as the Thessalonian letters of Paul. Anyone familiar with New Testament literature knows that the Thessalonian letters—particularly the first one—are concerned with the fact that death has taken some Christians away; that the expected return of the Saviour has not come off. Beyond this is the traditional belief that Mark's Gospel was written shortly after Peter's death, and was possibly inspired by it. So death is a genuine concern all through the Christian church.

Paul deals with that concern by homing in on the resurrection hope (1 Thess. 4:13-18); Mark addresses his Gospel to that question by including this lovely story. Perhaps the key sentence is Jesus' word: "She is not dead, but sleeping."

Is Mark quietly saying that though death seems to have an unrelenting finality about it, reality belies the appearance? Death may seem to be an impenetrable wall, but Jesus has put a door in that wall. The grave may be a darkness, but Jesus has cast a light in that darkness.

The New Testament continually speaks of death as a sleep. At the end of Stephen's terrible martyrdom, he fell asleep. David, after he had served his day and generation, fell asleep. Among the Corinthians, many sleep. Some of those who were witnesses of the resurrection are now asleep. Those who have died have fallen asleep. The dead are those who sleep in Christ (Acts 7:60; 13:36; 1 Cor. 11:30; 15:6,18,20; 1 Thess. 4:13-15).

Sleep is something from which we awake to live more strongly. An old warrior's ballad says, "I'll lay me down to rest awhile and then I'll fight again." All through the New Testament is this certainty that death is not the finality it seems but a sleep. Mark is saying, with John Ruskin, "Do not wear black for the guests of God." The sorrow of death must be for the death those who have died have done us.

As O. Henry lay dying of tuberculosis in a poor lodging house, a few friends gathered about him. Seeing that the end was near, one stepped to the flaring gas jet and started to lower the flame. O. Henry lifted a weak hand and said, "Do not turn out the light; I am afraid to go home in the dark."

Perhaps Mark is quietly assuring us that death has not turned out the light; that we need not go home in the dark. In this— as in all else—you are too important to be forever eclipsed.

Notes

1. Barclay, *And He Had Compassion on Them,* p. 60.
2. Adapted from Mrs. F. C. Burroughs, "Transformed," in *Rodeheaver's Gospel Songs* (Philadelphia: The Rodeheaver Co., 1922), p. 11.

10 Religious Unbelievers

Mark 6:1-6

Some time ago Louis Cassels of United Press International gave nation-wide publicity to a finding of the Survey Research Center of the University of California. His first sentence read, "There may not be any atheists in foxholes, but there are some in churches." In a sampling taken of more than three thousand church members it was discovered that there is a dull-edged conviction on some of the basic tenets of the Christian faith. Here are some of the findings:

Twenty-nine out of every one hundred Protestants questioned were not sure they believed in God, although seven of the twenty-nine did go as far as to say they thought there was a "higher power." One of every one hundred was frank enough to confess, "I don't know whether there is a God and I don't believe there is any way to find out."

On such questions as the deity of Christ, the virgin birth, and the after-life, there was similar uncertainty. Twenty-four out of every one hundred Protestants could only profess belief that Christ's promise of eternal life is "probably true."

Apparently, much of the religion practiced in our modern America is on the part of unbelievers. Now we might be shocked at this, if we could think it is something new. But Mark's Gospel suggests that this is nothing new; it is as old as the hills, at least as old as the first-century contemporaries of Jesus.

One of the themes which lies quietly in the writing of Mark is how the gospel of Jesus was stifled by hostile surroundings. There was a tendency not to believe, even on the part of the disciples. Jesus contended with this constantly.

Our Scripture story is a small sampling of the general climate of unbelief in which Jesus worked; it draws the curtain on the kind of malignant agnosticism through which Jesus was compelled to draw his disciples into the deeper commitment.

As we unfold the drama of Jesus' conflict with this prevalent agnosticism, we see reflected something of our own reservations and hesitancies. We cannot really see the struggle of the disciples without seeing our own struggle, too. Perhaps the movement of their hearts from unbelief to faith can be the catalyst for our own journey. Were we to divide our thoughts drawn from the story they would be in three parts: first, unbelief; then the dawning splendor; and finally, the recovery of glory.

Unbelief

Up to now Mark has been telling us of the wonders Jesus did; here it is of the wonders he did *not* do. The reason given is unbelief: the unbelief of the people in the Saviour's hometown.

Now a very natural question emerges: What was it they did not believe in—Jesus, or his power to work wonders? Or was it something more fundamental?

There is a clear indication that Jesus' townsmen had their doubts about him. After all, they knew him well—his family, his trade, his educational limitations. That part of it we cannot dismiss lightly. It is an all-too-human trait to permit proximity to breed contempt. And these people of Nazareth were contemptuous of Jesus, to be sure.

Is there more here than meets the eye? If this attitude of scorn was not only toward Jesus but toward the whole idea of God's moving in such a common prosaic way in their midst, then the whole episode is cast in a new light. This is exactly what we have. The men and women of Nazareth could not help but smirk at the very suggestion that God might penetrate their tightly structured little world in the person of anyone—much less this carpenter. Like Julian the Apostate, they asked one another, "Just what has this carpenter been doing lately?" They could not believe he was building coffins for emperors, and indeed, for the whole domain of evil. They just did not have a God like that; a God who would get "familiar" with his world; a God who would break into life in such a practical, meaningful way. It was too good to be true. In short, it was unbelievable.

The unbelief of Nazareth, like the unbelief in our churches today, centers in the kind of God we have. J. B. Phillips puts the problem to us clearly:

The trouble with many people today is that they have not found a God big enough for modern needs. While their experience of life has grown in a score of directions, and their mental horizons have been expanded to the point of bewilderment by world events and by scientific discoveries, their ideas of God have remained largely static. It is obviously impossible for an adult to worship the conception of God that exists in the mind of a child of Sunday School age, unless he is prepared to deny his own experience of life. If, by a great effort of will, he does do this he will always be secretly afraid, lest some new truth may expose the juvenility of his faith. And it will always be by such an effort that he either worships or serves a God who is really too small to command his adult loyalty.[1]

Dr. Phillips then goes on to enumerate in an interesting and disturbing fashion some of the concepts of God that are too small to meet our needs: "Resident Policeman, Grand Old Man, Heavenly Bosom, Managing Director, Secondhand God, Pale Galilean, and so on. But I suspect that if we were to get at the root of the problem which Dr. Phillips discusses so imaginatively, it would simply be that we have whittled God down in order that we might be God ourselves. The Old Tempter still whispers, "You shall be as gods," and we like it.

It is not too hard to believe in our Godlikeness. When one man can cut out the heart of another man, lay it out on a table, and while others hook up a heart-lung machine, repair the original organ, putting it back in and hooking it up so that it works like new, it is easy to entertain Godlike thoughts about him. When you add to his medical wonders his probings into the secret of the inner space of the atom and the outer space of the universe, the whole idea of God seems to shrivel.

So this struggle in belief-unbelief is essentially a struggle over who is going to be God. Not long ago I had a conversation with a young medical student. He frankly confessed that he had been bothered by some deep philosophical problems, introduced by his studies. He was candid enough to say to me—not as a preacher, but as a friend—that he was at sea as far as belief was concerned. In response, I said something like this:

The fundamental question is an approach to life. We must begin at one of two points: Either we believe in God and go from there, or we disbelieve and go from there. One is the theist. The other the atheist.

If you are a theist, then you must ask, how does God reveal himself? Christianity replies, "God reveals himself supremely in Jesus Christ. He comes in the only form we know—the human form; he speaks the only language we know—the language of human experience; he defeats the only real enemy we have—the enemy death."

To decide whether you are going to be a theist or an atheist, project your own life out to the last hour. In that hour you face certain questions, which I would put like this: Have I lost anything by being a Christian that I would have gained by being non-Christian? Is there any dimension of joy, of hope, of integrity that being non-Christian might have added? And, of course, the answer is no. You have gained all that in this life, and the Christian hope is added besides.

If, on the other hand, your basic approach has been one of unbelief, what have you gained? Nothing. And if Christianity be true, what have you lost? You have lost it all.

Without ever saying it, Mark shows us how Jesus is making this clear to his disciples. In a climate of malignant unbelief, he is showing the loss that comes by succumbing to our surroundings. Perhaps that is what Mark means by the remark, "He could do no mighty work there, . . . because of their unbelief" (6:5-6, RSV).

The Dawning Splendor

A good storyteller would not leave the issue unresolved. Mark is a consummate reporter, as well as editor. We could trace the issue out through Mark, except there is disagreement among the scholars as to just how Mark ends the story. Fortunately we need not enter the quarrel; we can simply turn to one of the men involved in the drama—the disciple John. In verse 14 of the first chapter of his Gospel he seems to put the whole issue in one terse phrase: "We saw his glory, such glory as befits the Father's only Son, full of grace and truth" (NEB).

We recognize this statement as a conclusion, a conclusion of belief. It is a kind of confession of faith. But the record is abundantly clear that this glory they saw came as a sunrise, with the final burst of light coming after the resurrection. They began to see the glory, the splendor of Jesus, and it grew and grew upon them. But it was a gradual thing.

We might ask, Just what was it they saw? And in reply we could say they saw in Jesus all the virtue, the goodness, the light they could have wished they might have found in themselves. They did not see the kind of glory the great of earth attempt to generate. In *The Edge of the Sword,* Charles de Gaulle speaks of that kind of glory:

He (the great man) must accept the loneliness which is "the wretchedness of superior beings." Contentment and tranquility and the simple joys which go by the name of happiness are denied to those who fill positions of great power. The choice must be made, and it is a hard one: whence that vague sense of melancholy which hangs about the skirts of majesty.[2]

That was not the kind of glory the disciples saw in Jesus. They saw in him an unpretentious authority, a goodness that was not self-conscious, a grand simplicity, and imperturbable equilibrium. In short, they saw in him all the things they could wish to see in themselves. His perfect manhood was the measure of their fall from glory. They saw in him the men they might have been, and it was enough. They finally came to believe. There was a point where those who saw this splendor, this glory, came to say, "The only explanation for this splendor is God! This life is—in a special way—the reflection of the original glory!"

The Recovery of Glory

Now all this is so much history—the history of an encounter of some persons with Jesus of Nazareth. Can it be anything more?

This is exactly the point of the whole passage. Mark wrote—as did John—for men and women who could never move through those dramatic, historic events. The Gospel of Mark was written as a kind of witness. It was written to say that life is not boxed in on all sides; that this life can take on a dimension of depth and meaning that can be described only by the word "glory" (2 Cor. 3:18).

The death of Paul Carlson, missionary in the Congo, seemed such a futile and ironic death. But consider the interpretation Dr. Paul's brother Dwight put on his death:

Despite the emotion that welled up in my heart when I heard of Paul's death, I was reminded of a statement that Mother made years ago: that God had given her each of her children. She had committed them to God. . . .

Paul went to the Congo not only for the humanitarian reason of alleviating physical suffering and pain through modern medicine, but, more important, to convey a message of hope in Christ.[3]

"To convey a message of hope in Christ." What is that hope? That in spite of the fearsome array of the powers of darkness in that land where he lived and worked, man had an essential glory to be reclaimed. That glory is found in Christ. Not in imitation of him, but in vital relationship with him—such as a vine with its branch (2 Cor. 3:18; John 15:5). This recoverable glory lifts a man out of darkness into light, out of death into life, out of despair into hope. And that hope outlasts the grave—for Paul Carlson, and for those who hear and heed the message, anywhere, anytime.

Notes

1. J. B. Phillips, *Your God Is Too Small* (New York: The Macmillan Co., 1961), p. 7.

2. Charles de Gaulle, in *The Edge of the Sword* (New York: Criterion Books, Inc., trans. Gerard Hopkins, 1960), as quoted in *Life*, Jan. 8, 1965.

3. Quoted in *Bible Society Record*, January, 1965, p. 5.

11 The Miracle That Never Happened

Mark 6:14-29

Our Scripture passage is authentic: a page torn from life as we know it. No more genuine event exists; it is true to the nature of this all-too-familiar, intact world. And it is a verifiable bit of history.

Up to this point in his narrative, Mark has told us of the miracles that Jesus worked, of the desperate circumstances he transformed. The one exception, of course, was the interlude in Nazareth where unbelief blocked anything exceptional.

But now we come on this historical footnote: the story of how John the Baptizer died. It is a sad story; a story where the ending is all wrong. It is a story where wrong prevails; where right goes down; where a miracle that was desperately needed never happened.

It all started when Herod Antipas—a son of Herod the Great who killed all the babies in Bethlehem—decided to take his new wife and stepdaughter down to his summer palace at Machaerus, near the Dead Sea. Now it would have been hot there in the summertime except for the elevation. It was more than three thousand feet above sea level. To make it even more attractive, there were all kinds of mineral springs around to keep the royal family in the pink.

There had been a little family trouble among the Herods of late. Herod Antipas, the hero of our story, had been in Rome not long before, visiting his brother Philip. While there, even though a married man, he took a shine to his brother's wife. Her name was Herodias. Therein we have the beginnings of a triangle—a rather complicated triangle. One of the complications was that this Herodias was not only Antipas' sister-in-law but also his niece. But kinship did not matter much to the Herods, and Antipas went to work on Herodias. He charmed her and flattered her until she finally gave in to him. Now that she had gone that far, she decided the only decent thing to do was to leave Philip and go with Antipas. So while Antipas hurried back to get a divorce from his legal wife, Herodias went to court in Rome. After a few hectic months and two divorces, Herodias came to live with Antipas, bringing her daughter (who was also Antipas' grandniece) with her. Things had been pretty tense for both of them, and that was the reason for the trip to the mineral baths at Machaerus.

Perhaps nothing would have come of it except for the fact that John the Baptist had been holding a brush arbor meeting in the Jordan Valley not too far from Herod's summer place. Since the doings of the great are matters of common conversation, John had some uncomplimentary things to say about the high-jinks going on at the palace. Word sifted back to the royal family, which prompted Herod to make a sly move: he invited John to the palace to preach.

Now this does not seem too unnatural when you remember that Herodias' grandmother was a daughter of one of the famous high priests of the Maccabean era. They were no strangers to priests, preachers, and the like. Besides, they wanted to hear firsthand what John had to say.

Now if John had had the discretion which is the better part of valour, he might have cut the pattern to suit the cloth. But John was made of sterner stuff. He took as his text for that court sermon Leviticus 18:16, which is graphic enough: "You shall not uncover the nakedness of your brother's wife" (RSV). He proceeded to preach on adultery. You may be sure he had no problem getting the attention of the court, nor did the court have any problem getting the message. Although Antipas could be philosophical about it all, Herodias took exception to the preacher's remarks. She made it so rough on her new husband that he had John put in the dungeon.

Things rocked along for a while without any change. Herodias was trying to persuade Antipas that this preacher should be put out of his misery. Antipas would call John up for a conference, discover he had not changed his mind at all on the sensitive subject of the royal marital affairs, and then send him back. Some-how Herod felt purer after he had talked with John, something like having the preacher get all over you when you go to church. All the while Herodias was watching her chances. She felt that if she could kill John she could quiet her own guilt feelings. One day, checking the calendar, Herodias got an inspiration. Her new husband was having a birthday soon. Why not have a birthday party? The plot began to take shape.

Well, the party was a real smash. Everybody got roaring drunk, ate until they had the stomachache and had that blah feeling.

Then Herodias made her bold move: she suggested that her nubilous, teen-age daughter dance for her husband's leery-eyed guests. The sheer daring of the move threw Herod off balance; he fell for it hook, line, and sinker. When lovely Salome did her dance it was apparent she had been doing her homework; never had royal flesh been bared more seductively. It set Herod and all his crowd on fire.

When at last Salome sank to the floor, head on knees and arms akimbo, her stepfather Antipas jumped to his feet and said expansively: "Tell me what you want! Anything up to half the kingdom," which was stretching a point since he was only a kind of governor. Salome said, "Oh, I don't want anything—much."

"What is it?" roared the drunk Herod. "What do you want?"

Then, with just the proper dash of modesty, she springs the trap. "Well, since you insist, just bring me that Preacher John's head on a platter." Just like that, the jig was up. Herodias had won. The deed was done. John was as good as dead.

Now somewhere in that sequence of events, John needed a miracle. It could have been a summer storm that blew the roof off. Or an earthquake. Or a volcano eruption (they had them down there once in a while). Or a mere stroke of apoplexy. Just any little old miracle would have done.

But nothing happened. Herod and his wife and daughter en-joyed perfect health, in spite of their debauchery. None of their guests got sick. The sun shone as though nothing had happened. The wind continued to whisper its caresses about Machaerus. And Jesus stayed up in Galilee, just about as far away from Machaerus as one could get and still be in the country. John needed a mir-acle but it never happened.

Now why did Mark include this story in his Gospel? And with miracles both before and after? Well, we know that it serves one purpose: it explains Jesus' withdrawal from Galilee, his more intensive training of the twelve and sending them out on their own. But is that all?

Perhaps we have to reflect on it a while, but it seems that Mark inserts this story with more purpose than to explain a shift of locale and strategy. The story of Antipas, Herodias, Salome, and John tells us at least three things: first, something about evil; then, something about good; and finally, something about God.

Something About Evil

This story unmasks the idea that evil is not real; that suffering and disease, death and anguish are all figments of the imagination. The three monkeys may sit with their hands respectively over ears, eyes, and mouth, saying they will see no evil, hear no evil, say no evil; but that does not destroy evil. Evil has a separate existence; its own design; a varied means.

It would not be unlikely that some would ask: How did it all start? Where did evil come from? The Greeks had an answer. They said it came from Pandora's box. But that is too pat, too artificial.

The Hebrews tell us it all started when our first parents decided that they could be gods on their own; they could exercise their freedom in rebellion rather than obedience. The Hebrews say that all this disorder is a distortion of the true order as the Father in heaven designed it and intended that it should remain. This corresponds to our own experience. For if our first parents were anything like we are, then it was easier to do wrong than right; to rebel than to obey. Our experience teaches us there is a genuine reality about evil.

For the truth about evil is that although it exists independently of us it also exists in us and works through us. To deny this is to deny ourselves.

> Ah me! we believe in evil,
>   Where once we believed in good;
> The world, the flesh, and the devil
>   Are easily understood.[1]

The evil that destroyed John began in Antipas and Herodias and Salome—each at a different point, but all intersecting in that bent, grotesque wisp of time when John's doom was sealed.

Where does evil begin with you and me? The same place. The New Testament warns: "Let no one say when he is tempted, 'I am tempted by God'; for God cannot be tempted with evil and he himself tempts no one; but each person is tempted when he is lured and enticed by his own desire. Then desire when it has conceived gives birth to sin; and sin when it is full-grown brings forth death" (James 1:13-15, RSV).

Something About Good

John teaches us something about good: it is a positive force. It resists evil; it struggles to overcome evil wherever it finds it, whether it be within the man or without. The struggle is not without its price. Dag Hammarskjold in his *Markings* has a few cryptic lines which were tragically fulfilled in his own death. They are lines that could be written about anyone who is committed to the good, as John was committed:

> Smiling, sincere, incorruptible—
> His body disciplined and limber.
> A man who had become what he could,
> And was what he was—
> Ready at any moment to gather everything
> Into one simple sacrifice.[2]

But how to be so aligned with good? That is the question. Dostoevski recognized in himself what some of us have yet to discover: that we are a mixture of good and evil. In his last novel, *The Brothers Karamazov,* the oldest of four sons of the elder Karamazov is Dmitry. He is a typical Dostoevskian mixture of good and bad: undisciplined and lustful at times; at other times rising to acts of piety and pure virtue.

Is not that true of us all? Studdert Kennedy read our pedigree aright when he wrote that man is a mixture. Part of him comes from heaven and part of him comes from earth.

The part of him that "comes from heaven" is the part of him that carries the breath of God. It is fragile; it needs help. But it can grow strong.

How? Not by mere self-discipline; not by self-laceration. Such an effort produced the Pharisees of Jesus' day. Every moral improvement hardens the core of pride. And pride is one of the cardinal sins.

It is more a matter of identification. Sometimes in our youth fellowships we sing:

> I have decided to follow Jesus
> No turning back; no turning back.

That is how this identification begins. It is a choice. Edwin Markham's "The Testing" tells us how important that choice is:

> I will leave man to make the fateful guess,
> Will leave him torn between the No and Yes,
> Leave him unresting till he rests in Me,
> Drawn upward by the choice that makes him free—
> Leave him in tragic loneliness to choose,
> With all in life to win or all to lose.

But the choice is only the beginning; it is the beginning of change. Dostoevski's Dmitry was charged with the murder of his father, although he was innocent. A tight chain of circumstantial evidence pointed toward his guilt. His past record of undisciplined life was against him. And in this crisis Dmitry faced up to the evil he had done in the past. He interpreted the unjust charge of murder as the suffering his past wrongs imposed. He determined to accept the suffering; to put his past in the hands of Christ; to give himself to the good. And if you know the story, then you know the change that came over him.

Or think of Peter. Such a bold coward! But change took hold, and at Pentecost he was no coward: he was the soul of courage. Peter had been stiffened by the resurrection-hope, and he could stand with the good, at any cost.

Peter is a clue for us. We cling steadfastly to the good when we believe that the good offers hope beyond anything this life can offer. So the New Testament speaks, "Every man that hath this hope in him purifieth himself" (1 John 3:3). The good holds a consummation so bright that we can stand any strain the good may impose upon us.

Something About God

In the story, the good of John and the evil of the Herods was locked in conflict; that much is apparent. But what of God? It would seem that God could not care less. John was left in the lurch. Or was he?

We need to remember that God does not "tell time" as we do. He has no clock and no calendars. God can take his eternity. It is when we impose our time-conditioned way of thinking upon the ways of God that we get all shook up. With God the end of time is not the end. Death is not a defeat; it is an elevation. We are lifted out of time's limits. We can begin to see the far horizons of eternity.

When John looked down from heaven upon Machaerus, the Herods, and Jesus, he saw an altogether different picture. Jesus—the Saviour—would also die; it was a part of man's redemption. But before Jesus would die, work had to be done with the followers who were to carry on. They were not yet ready.

Any miracle against Herod would have been a miracle of king-size proportions. It would have to be. And it would do nothing to get the disciples ready for the death of Jesus. It would only cloud the issue. It would obscure the mission. It would make things harder.

So God *had* taken a walk: a walk down into time—in the person of Jesus. As a matter of fact, God was getting ready to die himself, and in that death all men would have hope of eternal life.

So Mark did not hesitate to put this little historical interlude in the story. It was a part of the plan. It was the miracle that did not happen because the Father had a much larger miracle in view: the reconciliation of the whole world to himself through the death of Jesus, his Son and our Saviour.

Notes

1. Adam Lindsay Gordon, "Wormwood and Nightshade," from *Poems of Adam Lindsay Gordon* (New York: Oxford University Press, 1946), stanza 8.

2. Dag Hammarskjold, *Markings*. Translated by Leif Sjoberg and W. H. Auden. Copyright 1964 by Alfred A. Knopf, Inc. and Faber and Faber Ltd. Used by permission.

12 Bread for the Hungry
Mark 6:30-44

When a miracle can summons four witnesses, there must be something special about it. None of the writers of the Gospel overlooks this story: it was too widely known, too popular. It comes down to us as having the best credentials and more complete detail than any other.

What makes this story so important? Why were the early Christians so impressed with it? Why did they love it so?

An interesting clue lies so securely hidden in the Scriptures that we are likely to read right past it. Mark and Matthew tell, not only of the feeding of five thousand, as do all the Gospel writers (cf. Matt. 14:17; Luke 9:13; John 6:9), but also of the feeding of a group of four thousand. Now the interesting thing about these similar accounts is not in their similarity but in their differences. One difference is geographic (one Jewish, the other Gentile); another is of symbols (the recurring number twelve in one, seven in the other); still another is in language (the Jewish word for basket in one, the Gentile word for basket in the other).[1]

Mark first wrote down both stories. He was a child of both worlds—Jewish and Gentile. His Gospel emerges after he served as interpreter for Peter, the eminent Jewish apostle, in a Gentile congregation. So the miracle addresses itself to a fundamental concern of both Jew and Gentile. But what is that concern?

This question might remain unanswered were it not for the apostle Paul. In his brilliant analysis of the two parts of the first-century world—Gentile and Jew—Paul bares the terrible despair that lay at the heart of every man (Rom. 1:18 to 3:20). For the Jew it was a despair brought on by moral impotence: he knew the Law but could not keep it. For the Gentile it was a despair brought on by moral perversion: he had a sense of the Law in his own conscience but could not fulfil it. So there was a dual distortion. The Jew, in attempting to be religious, was a Pharisee. The Gentile, in attempting to be religious, was a pervert. Both were caught in a spiral of despair.

So the monotheism of the Jew and the polytheism of the Gentile both led to the same place—despair. Their religion left them with an aching void in their lives. Each in his own way suffered from a desperate spiritual hunger.

Then it begins to dawn on us why, for both Jewish and Gentile Christians, this story of the feeding of the multitudes would have special appeal. It is the story of bread for the hungry; it seems to catch up in symbol the reality of their own experience in Christ. It was a graphic way of telling what Christ meant to them in their own experience.

Jesus and the Hungry

The first fact of the story is obvious: the crowds were hungry. This was in the days of Jesus' popularity; in fact, he was riding the crest. His popularity was a genuine problem. He could not get away from his admirers. That is how the whole thing happened.

Details of the procedure in organization are clear enough; it is the details of the miracle that are missing. And when you reflect on it a little, you are grateful. The restraint of the Gospel writers from giving us a step-by-step description of the miracle itself leaves room for every age to fill in its own details. The fact that remains is that the Father met the needs of that hungry crowd when Jesus broke bread for them. And the retelling of the story was the means of freshening faith.

Of course, the hunger of those who had come to love the story was different. It was the hunger of despair.

What is our hunger today?

A research analyst searched out the happiest, most contented people in America and found them to be (1) young, (2) wealthy, (3) healthy, and (4) married. For one reason or another most of us would have our own private reason for discontent, according to that formula. If our hunger *is* for happiness, and we do not have a happy marriage, or wealth, or health, or youth— a likely prospect, since we belong to the aging human race—then are we to assume that life holds nothing for us? Perhaps Shakespeare's Macbeth is right:

Out, out, brief candle!
Life's but a walking shadow, a poor player
That struts and frets his hour upon the stage
And then is heard no more. It is a tale
Told by an idiot, full of sound and fury,
Signifying nothing. (Act 5, Scene 5)

Yet, we cannot let the question die with that. The hunger for a better answer is too deep. Even youth (one of the requirements for happiness) feels the quiet discontent that insists on a better answer. Not long ago in an informal talk to faculty members of our university, Walter Judd gave evidence of that. He told of how he had been invited to participate in a colloquy comprising about fifteen hundred students from the Ivy League schools of the East—Amherst, Holyoke, Yale, Vasser, Harvard. These students had drawn up a statement of concern, several paragraphs long, in which they set out the tensions between our controlled society and the individual man. It was all quite academic. But that was not all that was on their minds.

Dr. Judd indicated that the real questions they were wanting to ask, and did ask, were: What is the meaning of life? What about right and wrong? What about death? "But like Nicodemus," said Dr. Judd, "they came to ask such questions when no one else was around; when nobody else would hear them. They were interested, but they were somewhat ashamed that they were interested."

Perhaps one student who was not quite so shy defined the hunger of many of the younger generation. She wrote of it in a nationally circulated magazine:

Our generation has been exposed, through every means of communication, to major and minor fears—the little threat of not finding a mate if one does not use a certain mouthwash, or fear of non-acceptance if one does not succumb to a low moral standard because it is "the nature of the beast."

Many of us accept the premises that "You can't fight City Hall," "Live life to its fullest now," so "Eat, drink and make Mary"—for tomorrow we will be destroyed by nuclear war.

I am old-fashioned enough to believe in God, to believe in the dignity and potential of His creature—man—and I am realistic, not idealistic, enough to know that I am not alone in these feelings.

Some say that unlike other generations we have no threat to our freedom, no cause to propagate, no mission in life—everything has been handed to us. We have not been pampered, but spiritually impoverished. I don't want to live in the poverty of affluence—and I cannot live alone.[2]

Spiritual hunger is not only for the youth. Those in middle life know this hunger, too. Like Abraham of old, who was obviously a man of some wealth in the great Chaldean city of Ur, we are stirred to restlessness. Or like the little girl, we stop jumping rope for a while. When asked why, we can only answer: "Suddenly it all seems so futile." Like Abraham we want more from religion and from life than a nice spread in Suburbia. We have a hunger that bread will never satisfy.

So perhaps, young, middle-aged, old, this story—if we will let it—can come alive again and speak to us.

Jesus and Bread

Bread is such an ordinary, plain thing. There is a tendency to be disdainful. But,

> There is so much beauty in bread—
> Beauty of sun and soil,
> Beauty of patient toil.
> Winds and rains have caressed it,
> Christ often blessed it.
> Be gentle when you touch bread.[3]

It was bread Jesus touched in this story to satisfy the needs of the multitude.

There are at least two things this part of the story tells us. First, we are assured that Jesus has a care for men's bodies. The gospel of Jesus calls for a balance. There is in the gospel an intense personal concern: a hope that is addressed to me as a person, one which is a never-to-be repeated event.

But in the gospel we find a social concern, too. There cross my desk several different publications put out by special interest groups. One of them carries the title "Christian Economics"; another "Date-line"; another "Life-line." Each of these in its own way sounds the note of hard-line, hard-nosed capitalism. It is laissez-faire, every man for himself, carried out to the highest power. And to the men who sponsor these propaganda sheets, the doctrine makes sense. Only one thing is wrong. They all overlook (even the one bearing the title "Christian") that Christ fed the multitudes, that Jesus' gospel has a social dimension. We may not want it. We may not like the involvement that surely goes along with it. But we do not dare deny it. This story tells us there is a social dimension to the gospel.

When General Booth began the work of the Salvation Army in London, he gave the people food, hot meals. Some people criticized him for this. They said that such was no part of the duty of a man who was out to win men to Christ. Booth replied: "How can you warm a man's heart with the love of Christ when his feet are cold?" This is the whole sphere of the gospel.

Since it is bread that is the means of Christ's work, we stumble on the realization that Christ's work is any work that is done in his Spirit. Nothing is too menial, too commonplace.

The housewife is right who has a plaque over her sink which reads, "Divine service held here three times every day." And so was Walter Judd when he advised a group of ministers and laymen: "The task of the minister is not to speak *for* the church, but to speak *to* the church. The task of the laymen is to take the truth of the church (or we might say gospel) and apply it to daily life."

Christ touches bread, and it begins to meet human need. He touches lives, and those lives also begin to meet human need wherever it is found. Remember Jesus' own test for the last judgment? "Inasmuch as ye did it unto one of these, ye did it unto me."

Jesus and the Living Presence

This lovely story was remembered because it symbolized the satisfaction of deep spiritual hungers in Jesus; because it baptized the common things of life. Yet, there is still another reason it had become a favorite. It might be stated this way: as the physical bread had brought nourishment to the multitudes when Jesus was among them in the body, so the spiritual bread brings nourishment to men and women when Christ is within.

Without this Living Presence in our life, everything goes flat. In a conversation with Eve, Adam tells how flat it can get:

"If only there may be an end some day, and yet no end! If only I can be relieved of the horror of having to endure myself forever! If only the care of this terrible garden may pass on to some other gardener! If only the sentinel set by the Voice can be relieved! If only the rest and sleep that enable me to bear it from day to day could grow after many days into an eternal rest, an eternal sleep, then I could face my days, however long they may last. Only, there must be some end; some end. I am not strong enough to bear eternity."[4]

That is life without spiritual bread, without the Living Presence. But there is a higher order of existence. For those who may be hungry there is bread. Matthew Arnold has a poem that tells the difference:

> 'Twas August, and the fierce sun overhead
> Smote on the squalid streets of Bethnal Green,
> And the pale weaver, through his windows seen
> In Spitalfields, look'd thrice dispirited.

> I met a preacher there I knew, and said:
> "Ill and o'erwork'd, how fare you in this scene?"
> "Bravely!" said he; "for I of late have been
> Much cheer'd with thoughts of Christ, the living bread."[5]

Notes

1. Richardson, *op. cit.,* p. 98.
2. "The Face of the Future," *Look,* January 12, 1965, p. 76.
3. "Bread," *Masterpieces of Religious Verse,* p. 495.
4. George B. Shaw, *Back to Methusaleh* (London: Constable & Co., 1931), p. 12.
5. Quoted in Barclay, *And He Had Compassion on Them,* p. 168.

13 Discovery

Mark 6:45-52

An explanation can be nailed together for the healing miracles; but what about the nature miracles: walking on water, calming a storm at sea, multiplying bread, turning water into wine? Ingenious efforts have been made to explain these, too: Jesus did not walk *on* the sea; he walked *by the sea.* Jesus did not actually feed the crowds; he gave them a dainty portion very much like the communion bread, and this was added to the lunches they already had. "The water turned into wine came at the end of the celebration," it is pointed out—with strong implication—that when you get so high and so happy you can't tell the difference between wine and water, anyhow.

Somehow such explanations do not enhance the miracles. They make them, and the men who wrote them, look cheap. Unless we remember that these miracles were first told, and then written, by men who had experienced the greatest of all miracles in their own hearts—reconciliation to the Father and an infusion of new moral power—we are likely to bog down in the details and the explanations and never push through to the real question: What are these men of faith saying?

Of this much we can be sure: the miracles are a witness about Jesus. They are eyewitness accounts, to be sure. But the accounts are given after the events and are more than mere journalistic reports. Meaning has been infused into the event; insight has come through faith; miracle has become no mere wonder—it is a means of gaining attention to convey truth. The sublime truth that lies in the very center of every story is the conviction that Jesus is something more. Here is a fourth dimension. To time, space, and person has been added the authentic revelation of God. But it is more than a revelation; it is the Father himself (John 10:30).

When we read the miracles not merely for the event but for the meaning, they take on a new luster, a new sparkle. Our present miracle story is a good example. It is a dual confession—a confession of spiritual blindness as well as a confession of faith. It is a faith that has been more than three decades in taking form and substance, for that is the time lapse between the event and the written report. But when we read the story, the faith that prompted it is in every line. Here is the mystery of the incarnation—one who is truly man and truly God, as the disciples experienced that mystery. The story begins by underlining the genuine humanity of Jesus. It continues with the sensory evidence of his essential deity and concludes with the report of this discovery.

The Essential Humanity

There is no more genuine picture of the essential humanity of Jesus than this one sentence: "After he had taken leave of them, he went into the hills to pray" (Mark 6:46, RSV). So complete was the humanity of Jesus that prayer was not only natural but indispensable.

One of the earliest heresies of the Christian faith—one whose shadow we find in the pages of the New Testament and lingering long after—denied the essential humanity of Jesus. These heretics were called Gnostics. They made the humanity of Jesus a fiction.

When Epaphras came to Rome to visit Paul in his prison cell, he reported to the veteran preacher that a new teaching had recently come into Colossae where he lived and ministered. Subtle, complex, and cloaked in mystery, it was called gnosticism. Epaphras did not know what to make of it. Much of it was attractive; it appealed to the intellectuals of his congregation. And yet, Epaphras had an intuitive sense of danger.

When he brought his report to Paul, the old warrior sprang into action. Where Epaphras had only an instinct, Paul had an insight. This was an attack upon the humanity of Jesus. This undercut everything that made Christianity unique and different. It could not be answered too swiftly. And in response to that movement in Colossae, Paul wrote his letter which we call Colossians. The key sentence of that letter is, "In him [Jesus] dwelleth all the fulness of the Godhead bodily" (2:9).

It is this genuine quality in the humanity of Jesus that gives us a theology for life—joys, sorrows; bright days, dark nights. If the humanity of Jesus were an illusory tissue, then we could have no confidence in stress and weakness. The virtue of a priest, or any minister, is his humanity. We take comfort in the knowledge that he understands because he also suffers. The virtue of our high priest is his humanity: "For we have not an high priest which cannot be touched with the feeling of our infirmities; but was in all points tempted like as we are, yet without sin. Let us therefore come boldly unto the throne of grace" (Heb. 4:15-16).

When we look at the Master in prayer, we find some of the most genuine moments of his humanity. This moment, when he was bone tired, is one of them. The disciples are slow about getting the feel of his mission. John the Baptizer—his cousin, and with whom he had more than a passing identification—lay the victim of Herod Antipas. The crowds, with their shallow expectations and wanting a miracle-worker who would make life easy for them, were pressing him. It was a moment that could only be met in prayer.

And then that sublime moment of all prayer moments when Jesus prayed, "Not my will, but thine." In *Christ and Human Suffering,* E. Stanley Jones writes of a night spent in the Garden of Gethsemane in which he tried to relive the experience of the Saviour when he prayed that prayer.

I expected to come away chastened, submissive, surrendered. But in those silent hours I found my thought shifting to the words of Jesus to the sleepy disciples: "Arise, let us be going"—let us be going to meet the betrayal, the rejection, the accusations, the spittle, the cross. . . . I came away with a battle-cry sounding in my heart.

Our humanity strikes a kindred note with the Saviour's humanity as we join him in these moments of prayer. So this miracle story begins with Jesus' returning to pray.

The Authentic Deity

Much of the New Testament is better understood if we have a firm grasp of the Old. And in the Old Testament, where God is revealed in the wonders of nature, a favorite means of picturing the power of God is in reference to the sea. When God wanted to deliver his people, he parted the sea. Even the lively sea could not swallow Jonah in the story of the prophet. You see, God was preserving him. One of the psalms has a graphic passage about God and the sea, the mere reading of which will throw light on our miracle story.

They that go down to the sea in ships, that do business in great waters; these see the works of the Lord, and his wonders in the deep. For he commandeth, and raiseth the stormy wind, which lifteth up the waves thereof. They mount up to the heaven, they go down again to the depths: their soul is melted because of trouble. They reel to and fro, and stagger like a drunken man, and are at their wit's end. Then they cry unto the Lord in their trouble, and he bringeth them out of their distresses. He maketh the storm a calm, so that the waves thereof are still. Then are they glad because they be quiet; so he bringeth them unto their desired haven (Psalm 107:23-30).

Steeped as they were in the images of the Old Testament, the disciples came to understand that the meaning of Jesus' coming to them on the water was so startling it was scarcely believable: Jesus was Lord of nature, an authentic evidence! Could it mean, just possibly, that here was one who was possessed of the power of God? They came to believe just that. Not all at once— even as the reporters tell us. But finally. And when the miracle story was written in, it was meant to be a confession of faith.

If one of the earliest controversies among Christians had to do with the humanity of Jesus, one of the liveliest had to do with his deity. It involved two emperors; the sudden death of one of the main debaters, Arius, about whom it is suggested that the excitement of having won a skirmish in the long battle brought on his death;[1] and both the Council of Nicaea (in 325) and the Council of Chalcedon (in 451). What was the consequence of all of this? It was finally agreed that Jesus was both "truly man and truly God."

Long before the councils settled themselves on the true identity of Jesus, these men who gave us our New Testament had settled it for themselves. The miracle story is a way of saying that Jesus had to be God. Who else but God could walk on water? This is no mere wonder: a defying of gravity; a demonstration of mind over matter. It is a witness. Jesus is God. He must be.

Blaise Pascal, the great French physicist and mathematician of seventeenth-century France, believed the miracles made an immeasurable difference. "I would not be a Christian," said he, "were it not for the miracles."[2]

The witness of this miracle story then is that Jesus is truly God.

Discovery

As we read these stories in our New Testament, they have a tendency to flatten out; there is a dimension of human experience that is missing. That is the dimension of time. What we must remember is that the Gospels—where we find these stories—were not written on the day the miracles happened. They were not even written the same year. The first one, Mark, was written somewhere between thirty-three and thirty-seven years after the event. Between the event and the report is a time lapse.

What was it in this time lapse that convinced the writers of our New Testament? What pieces of evidence were added that confirmed all the earlier holy suspicions?

For one thing there was the *crucifixion*. One thing they knew for sure: Jesus did not have to die as he did. He could have made himself scarce. He could have disappeared, and that would have been the end of it. The whole bit would simply have faded away.

There could only be one reason he went to a cross as he did, and suffered there: he loved them. Better than any man could love, Jesus loved them.

"The world is sick," said the voice, "for dirth of crucifixions.
Men give houses to those who hate them and country estates
    to those who spit on them.
They crucify only those who love them."[3]

Wallace Petty tells of taking a young ministerial student to hear Kagawa, when the great Japanese Christian was in America. As they were leaving, the young student remarked that he was disappointed. "You must admit there were not any new thoughts which were fresh and stimulating. Just a few worn-out cliches." Dr. Petty said nothing; and, as they walked along, the student continued, "I did, however, notice one thing. Kagawa wore heavy lenses on his glasses. Didn't I read that he developed trachoma down in the slums as he ministered to the physical and spiritual needs of his people?" As Dr. Petty, still wordless, smiled, the student said, "I guess I'm wrong. *After all, when a man is hanging on a cross he doesn't have to say very much."*[4]

And there was the *resurrection.* This solid piece of evidence could not be gainsaid. Neither stone nor soldier could prevent it.

And then there was the continuing life of Jesus, his abiding presence, in the church. She just would not die. The more men opposed her, the stronger she was. When the ax fell, the torch touched to the faggots, blood was spilled, to be sure. But out of that blood sprang more convinced Christians, and it became a saying: "The blood of the martyrs is the seed of the church."

These were the ingredients of the time lapse. They helped bring the discovery to something more than a tentative conclusion. They brought it to a faith; a faith to live by, and a faith to die in.

Is that not what Jesus meant by his story of the man who found a treasure hid in the field? So enthralled was he in this discovery—so overjoyed—that he rid himself of *everything,* just to possess the field and the treasure. The joy of his discovery cast all else in a new light. That is the missing note of much of our modern Christianity. The joyous abandon of discovery has thinned out to a dull habit or, even worse, a distasteful duty. The sad truth is that what passes for Christianity in our day is all too often nothing more than cultural conformity. Kierkegaard lamented the Christianity of his Denmark a hundred years ago, and it would well be the lament said over modern American Christianity:

It is the tolerance of the orthodox which best shows how completely Christianity is lost. Their solution is: if only we may keep our faith to ourselves, the world can take care of itself. Merciful God, and that is supposed to be Christianity. That is the power which once broke upon the world and through readiness to suffer forced Christianity on the world, compelled it more forcefully than any tyrant.

The orthodox do not even suspect that this, their tolerance, is the effect of sheer worldliness, because they have not really either understanding, respect or courage for martyrdom or a true belief in eternity, but really desire to have a good time in this world. . . .

How low has Christianity sunk, how powerless and miserable it has become![5]

If we can move behind this culture-brand, which so often passes for Christianity, and move to the Christ who began it all; if we can give ourselves to the quest and the discovery, then we shall know who Jesus really is. The disciples did that, over a period long enough to be a generation, and these miracles written down for us are a sublime and artful way of telling us of their discovery.

What is the discovery? That Jesus, whose humanity was so apparent as to be undeniable, was truly God; that his death and resurrection, his living presence in the church, confirmed their holy surmise of the distant bygone years: namely, that Jesus was their Saviour and Lord.

It would be difficult to put this truth more beautifully than Albert Schweitzer has already put it:

He comes to us as One unknown, without a name, as of old, by the lakeside, He came to those men who knew Him not. He speaks to us the same word: "Follow thou Me!" and sets us to the tasks which he has to fulfill for our time. He commands. And to those who obey Him, whether they be wise or simple, He will reveal Himself in the toils, the conflicts, the sufferings which they shall pass through in His fellowship, and, as an ineffable mystery, they shall learn in their own experience Who He is.[6]

Notes

1. See Williston Walker, *A History of the Christian Church* (New York: Charles Scribner's Sons, 1918), p. 119.

2. *The Reader's Companion to World Literature* (A Mentor Book, published by The New American Library), pp. 334-36.

3. Hermann Hagedorn, *The Bomb That Fell on America* (Santa Barbara, California: Pacific Coast Publishing Co., 1946).

4. Fred Wood, *Bible Truth in Person* (Nashville: Broadman Press, 1965), p. 123.

5. *The Journals of Kierkegaard, op. cit.,* p. 173.

6. Albert Schweitzer, *The Quest of the Historical Jesus* (London: A. & C. Black, Ltd., 1922), p. 401.

14 *Emancipation* *Proclamation*
Mark 7:24-30

Two miracles comprise this story: one obvious; the other obscure. The obvious miracle is the cure of the Syrophoenecian woman's daughter; the obscure miracle is the emancipation of the Gentile mother from the burden of racial and cultural discrimination. The former miracle is a witness to the power of the Saviour; the latter is a witness to the power of the Saviour's gospel.

The story opens in Gentile territory. In distance it is just a few miles to Galilee; in deities and devotion it is a world apart. The woman of the story is of Gentile extraction. Matthew identifies her as a Canaanite. Mark calls her "a Greek, a Syrophoenecian by birth." She could not have had a more antagonizing ancestry. She was one of the daughters of the Phoenecians, whose racial and cultural heritage ran back to the heathen Canaanites. I have been where her people once went to worship. Theirs was a religion of gross immorality. Huge pilasters, phallic symbols of the fertility cults, dominate the scene. Sympathetic magic and symbolic fertility rites were the prominent features of a religion that sought to manipulate the forces of an impersonal nature. The God she knew was capricious, immoral, and dwelt in the shadows. Her world and her life had little light cast upon it from her religion.

It is in this land of darkness that the gospel breaks off the chains of racial and cultural provincialism, reaching across the barriers that divide the Father's family, emancipating both the gospel and the woman of the story.

Quietly lying here in this story is the witness of the early Christians to the reach of the gospel. It has an external as well as an internal reach.

The External Reach

The clue that opens the story for us is the simple historical fact, as found in the book of Acts and the Pauline letters, that this Gospel was set down in a period when racial and cultural tensions were tearing at the very life of the church. The conflict just could not have been much more intense, short of open warfare. It had all the aspects of guerilla war—the devious stratagems, the suspicion and distrust, the sniping, as well as the undercover demolitions.

We discover from Paul's letter to the Philippians (written while a prisoner in Rome) that some were positively gleeful when his preaching had been thus curtailed. And while he was detained, they were vigorously pressing their rigid, confined, culture-bound brand of Christianity (1:15-18). The Jerusalem conference (which considered the whole question of Gentile admission into the church), the hypocritical dissimulation of Peter and Barnabas in Syrian Antioch (Acts 15: Gal. 2) were all events that had occurred in the past decade and a half. The openness of the church, the scope of the gospel—these were still live issues when this Gospel was set down.

But really, and this is the point of the story as it relates to this issue, the conflict was over a question already settled. Jesus had settled it. He had given the gospel to the Gentiles: here was one incident to prove it.

Not that it was easy for Jesus. The story manages to incorporate something of the struggle involved. We can sense it even as we follow the conversation given in our Scripture passage. Caught up in the storyteller's art is the tense issue still raging: is the gospel big enough to break out of the confines of race and culture? Is it big enough to bring to the human family the emancipation it so desperately needs? This event is the answer to all such questions.

That this was a question for the church in the first century is clear enough. It is a question for the church in the twentieth century as well. The shame of the church in America since World War II is that she has been one of the last rather than one of the first to face the issue of race and culture conflicts in our own nation.

American Christianity has its sectors. We can understand, and even appreciate, the denominational divisions. They are rooted in doctrine and in an understanding of the Scriptures. But what of the color divisions? They are rooted in race, in culture.

It was the men on the Negro side of the barrier who first

conceived of using the weapon of passive resistance. This they learned from Jesus. They had seen how effective it was in the hand of Ghandi, the little David of India, as he opposed the Philistine Goliath, Britain. And learning from him, American Negroes went to jail to protest the injustices written into our laws.

Then the political leaders recognized their cause as a moral issue, and we had the strange spectacle of religious and spiritual leaders' being asked by political leaders to recognize that the Negro cause was rooted in the gospel's estimate of every man.

Not that the ministry did not know that. Most of us were painfully aware, and struggling to find ways to register our convictions where it would help the cause—not make it hopeless. But we found it difficult to tell the men and women who paid the salaries that fed and educated our children how wrong it was to deny a man, for whom Christ died, the right to eat where he wanted to and to vote when he wanted to. There has been genuine anguish, soul-searching, and quiet heroism in the past decade in the ministry, particularly in the South.

The issue is still with us. Jesus settled it, but have we? Or are we one who "with death in his eyes, comes walking slowly and sees the shadow of death in many faces"?[1]

It is more than coincidental that Mark places in juxtaposition to this story of the Syrophoenecian woman an account of the resistance of the Pharisees to Jesus. We cannot help but see the contrast between their rigid, closed system which could find only a threat in Jesus and the openness of the Gentile woman who saw only a hope in him.

Is the church so much like the Pharisees that we can only huddle within the tight little enclosure we have erected for ourselves? Are there no windows and no doors that open onto the needs of all the world? Do we preach the gospel one way and put it into practice another?

The miracle story is put here to remind us that the gospel reaches far and wide; that in Christ the barriers and hostilities are all broken down. The New Testament says that beautifully, and we had better believe and practice it:

In Christ Jesus you who once were far off have been brought near in the blood of Christ. For he is our peace, who has made us both one, and has broken down the dividing wall of hostility, by abolishing in his flesh the law of commandments and ordinances, that he might create in himself one new man in place of the two, so making peace, and might reconcile us both to God in one body through the cross, thereby bringing the hostility to an end. And he came and preached peace (Eph. 2:13-17, RSV).

The Internal Reach

There is an emancipation of the church in this story, but there is more. There is also the emancipation of the Syrophoenecian woman.

To begin with, this little Syrophoenecian woman lived in the very center of a complex of stress-producing forces. Life had handed her a pretty bitter pill.

For one thing, her daughter was possessed of a demon. I am writing to the parents of a good many teen-agers who might think they have some knowledge of what that is like. But the turbulence in this mother-daughter relationship was not the normal tensions of growing up. Here was a girl who was vexed with a disabling disorder. There was no hope of improvement. The mother could not brush her brow and say, "Well, she'll outgrow it." It was a permanent condition. And her powers to cope with the present were not strengthened by hope for the future.

Beyond the condition of the daughter was a life situation that imposed very real vexations. Consider a life made up of these ingredients: poverty, illness, social inferiority, hopelessness. Then add the absence of any real, vital religious faith. Every day of her life was a numbing exposure to blind forces, all of them beating and pushing this courageous little woman down.

Have you ever had the feeling that the events of your life could better be understood in terms of a blind fate than a loving Heavenly Father? Then you can enter into the frustration of this woman. You may be a little like the beat, slouched, dejected seven-year-old boy who stood in front of the teacher's desk, hands crammed in his pockets. The teacher was examining a paper he had just handed her. Then, looking up, she said, "I'm sorry, Winslow, but I can't accept your resignation."

Beyond the harshness of life that made her its prisoner, there was this grinding, sometimes infuriating system of discrimination.

It was based on race and culture. If one accepted it he had to believe he was a second-class human being; if he did not accept it he had to live in a world where a lot of people did believe such. And the Jews were especially bad about that. Habitually they called these Gentiles "dogs."

Now that makes us face up to the question of Jesus' use of that very term in speaking to this woman. How did Jesus utter the word "dogs"?

Matthew's account suggests that Jesus had to think through a definition of his own mission—whether it was for the Jews alone or for the whole world. If that is true, then in the crisis of this experience, Jesus focused on the world.

In Mark's account there is no hint that Jesus was perplexed about the scope of the gospel, none at all. If we follow Mark we can imagine Jesus' saying, " 'Let the children first be fed, for it is not right to take the children's bread and throw it to the dogs' " (7:27, RSV), and winking as he said that word "dogs." By his inflection and the wink of the eye, Jesus demonstrated an attitude of derision, not toward the woman, but toward the absurd assumption that some of the Heavenly Father's children were less loved—that some of them had a lesser place in the Father's heart.

Even human parents know better than to believe such absurdity. Our own love for all our children teaches us better. Mrs. Eisenhower, mother of our twenty-ninth president, brings this into focus. When her famous warrior son was returning to his native Kansas after the victory in Africa and Europe, she awaited his arrival at the airport. With her were some of her other sons and members of their families. A reporter, interviewing the General's mother, asked the kind of inane question reporters can sometimes ask: "Mrs. Eisenhower, what do you think of your son?"

"Which one?" asked the mother.

"Which one?" To a mother, every boy she birthed is a son; every boy is precious; every boy is loved in his own right. Can it be less with the Father in heaven?

This dear little insignificant child of the Heavenly Father knew instinctively it was not. So, when she caught the Saviour's wink, she also caught its meaning. She knew that she was a *person* in Jesus' eyes, not a dog. And with a natural wit she made a perfect response: "Yes, but even the dogs under the table eat the children's crumbs." With that little byplay the chains of discrimination were struck a lethal blow.

In Ibsen's play *Peer Gynt* there is a striking scene when Peer Gynt makes his escape from the Kingdom of the Trolls. The Troll King says, "There were women praying for him. He was too strong for us."

There are always trolls to shackle us. But Jesus looks upon these trolls, whether they are internal or external, with a knowing eye. In him is the eternal yes of God. In him is emancipation! And if we are free in him, then we are truly free, and we accept the responsibilities that freedom brings.

There is a legendary story of a liberated slave who came to see President Lincoln. He insisted that he would not take his freedom as a gift, but proposed to pay for it. He threw a silver dollar on the President's desk. The kindly Mr. Lincoln tried to show the man that he could not buy his liberty; that the very fact he thought he could indicated he did not fully appreciate the priceless gift. When the freed slave insisted, the President took him to the window and showed him the row on row of soldier's graves in Arlington. Then the President taught the newly-freed man: "Your money cannot buy back the lives that have been given as the price of your freedom. You must go out and walk the world with gratitude, and live like a free man must."

We have been emancipated by Christ, who was a Jew. Mark has woven this little story into his Gospel to tell us that we must go out and walk the world with gratitude, and live as free men must.

Notes

1. Conrad Aikens, "The House of Dust," in *Selected Poems* (New York: Charles Scribner's Sons, 1931), p. 117.

15 Deaf and Dumb

Mark 7:31-37

Deafness is a symbol with significance far deeper than the mere matter of receiving and decoding messages. The miracle of restoration for the deaf-mute is a dramatic means the gospel writer employs to depict the struggle Jesus was having with his disciples. After Mark tells the story, he puts the problem very directly in a conversation Jesus has with the twelve: " 'Do you not yet perceive or understand? Are your hearts hardened? Having eyes do you not see, and having ears do you not hear?' " (8:17-18, RSV).

But that comes a little later. Here Jesus is acting out this problem. The deaf-mute provides the perfect opportunity. As Jesus employs these homely and personal means of unstopping the deaf ears and loosening the jammed-up tongue, he is symbolically portraying the miracle, on a far higher level, that has to take place with his own disciples if they are ever going to be ready to carry on after his ministry is over. The whole miracle is a kind of prayer of our Saviour for these disciples who are deaf to the heavenly import of what is going on, and therefore dumb to declare it.

Now when you reflect on the story and its setting, it comes to you that this whole business has a strange familiarity to it. Somehow, ever since Eden, it has been easier for us to hear and understand the voices of earth than the voices of heaven. We get deaf to the Father's voice quite early. We are not very old before we cease to talk of heavenly things. We may think about them; we seldom talk about them. Gamaliel Brandford, in his poem titled "Persistent," makes a confession for us all:

> I think about God,
>> Yet I talk of small matters
> Now isn't it odd
>> How my idle tongue chatters?

Of quarrelsome neighbors,
Fine weather and rain,
Indifferent labors,
Indifferent pain.

Some trivial style,
Fashion shifts with a nod;
And yet all the while
I am thinking of God.

To know just how true this is, let me pose a question: How long has it been since you had a good, long conversation with your mate—or your child—about such things as your own inadequacies at prayer; your own thoughts about the fundamental mysteries of life; your own guilt feelings?

Most of us will admit that we are pretty dumb about such things. Are we also deaf, like the disciples? Perhaps if we move in on the story we shall find some clues that will unravel our own dilemma. Let me suggest three: first, other voices; second, a strategy; third, a clear witness.

Other Voices

Have you ever really considered the veritable babble of voices we all hear seven days a week? These voices urge us to buy, to sell, to go, to stay, to spend, to borrow. Not only is it a babble; it is a confusion.

We can scarcely know our own minds.

These other voices emerge out of the world in which we live, and are all very much a part of it. In the disciples' day, these other voices had pretty well formed for them an image of the Messiah and his kingdom. Everything Jesus said and did was filtered through these expectations; they never really got an ungarbled message. The Jewish culture of their day—the common ideas and values—comprised a filter through which everything in Jesus' message had to move. They got little (if any) of the true import.

Now the kingdom of the average American is a little different from the disciples' kingdom. For one thing, it is not a dim and distant hope; it is a present possibility. Someone has pointed out that the average American family lives like kings now. Kings of the seventeenth century did not have running water, hot and cold;

air-conditioned homes, offices, automobiles, radios, televisions, telephones. They never rode in an airplane. And for all their wealth, the great European monarchs of the past lived less like kings than we do. The things we count necessities, such as central air-conditioning, they never heard of.

But there is a catch here. Constantly new conveniences are coming on the market. We are caught in the dilemma that one simple mountain man disdained. President Hutchins of Berea College tells his story. In a mountain store he saw a bunch of bananas for the first time. The storekeeper invited the man to eat one. "No, I ain't going to," said the old man.

"Why? Why not?"

"Well," said the old man, "I got so many tastes now I can't satisfy, I ain't going to add no more fancy ones to it."

Unless you stayed in bed today, you received about fifteen hundred impressions to do something—buy, sell, save, spend, hurry, relax, etc. Some of these impressions scored a direct hit with you. You bought a product because today, last week, or last year you formed an opinion that the product had more to offer than its competitors. Forming this opinion may have been the result of an advertisement, a testimonial from a friend, or a careful study of a promotional brochure. Or it may have been a combination of several different impressions.

Attempts to impress you cost producers ten billion dollars last year. They hired some of the best minds available to determine possible hidden resistance to their product and advertising copy. Topflight artists illustrated their ads. Expert media analysts helped select the vehicle to bring the message to you.

So advanced are the techniques for molding opinions in favor of products that social scientists and psychiatrists now help plan promotional efforts to engineer approval. Motivation research is uncovering new ways for producers to peddle their wares. Yet we read their ads and buy their products without knowing why.

Changing Times took notice recently of the fact that here in America in the past twenty-five years aspirin consumption has increased twice as fast as the population. The editor commented: "It figures—more TV sets, cars, and debts per person and more headaches per head."

All this so-called progress has exacted its pound of flesh. Five nations lead the world in alcoholism, a high divorce rate, juvenile delinquency, and mental illness. These nations are the United States, Switzerland, Britain, Denmark, and France. These are the western nations that also enjoy the highest standards of living. Could it be that there is some connection?

Physically, we are advancing. Every day there is a better chance we will live longer. We have improved social skills. And we are intellectually gifted. Any generation that can invent something to wipe out civilization isn't stupid. But the prevailing mood is that we are specks thrown out on a third-rate star by the accident of genetics and geophysics, and that life is empty, without any meaning or purpose.

Someone has suggested that the clue to understanding a culture is its advertisements. If that be true, then the wavelength that gets to the average modern American is sex, alcohol, and nonsense jingles. Even when advertising approaches the level of sanity, we are invited to sell our souls for a mess of pottage that goes snap, crackle, and pop.

Is it any wonder that we never hear from heaven? Our spirits lie stunned, battered, and inert. All these voices and claims are simply more than we can handle.

A Strategy

The second clue in the story predicts a strategy that Jesus would soon employ with his own disciples: The Saviour took the deaf man aside, out of the crowd. (Later on Jesus took the disciples away from the clamor and distractions of the crowd, too.) Could it be that the Gospel story is quietly saying something to us in this? Is this the suggestion of a strategy?

Perhaps the brilliant French scientist and Christian philosopher Pascal had something when three hundred years ago he said, "All the troubles of man come from his not knowing how to sit still." If Whirl is king, then Chaos is his kingdom. When haste is our best virtue, it is our values that get lost, and soon *we* are lost in what T. S. Eliot properly called "A Waste Land." He described it pretty well:

> And now you live dispersed on ribbon roads,
> And no man knows or cares who is his neighbour

> Unless his neighbour makes too much disturbance,
> But all dash to and fro in motor cars,
> Familiar with the roads and settled nowhere.[1]

If we sit still for a little while, our souls may have a chance to catch up with us. And when that happens, we are going to sort and sift these clamoring voices out, deciphering and decoding, trying to determine which ones are worth listening to. Now we've all had a crack at that at one time or another. It may have been a time of illness, or perhaps death, or some other emergency. Suddenly, we were brought up short and faced with the question: What goes on here? We began to look at the things we were doling out our lives for, and some of them were pretty silly. Probably we came to a conclusion right then that what we really needed to do was to rearrange our whole scheme of values. We had tumbled into the maze where absolute commitments were being given to relative values; that is, we were more careful about our attendance at the Kiwanis and Rotary meetings than we were about prayer meeting. We were better informed on foreign affairs than we were on church affairs. And as we look back on it, we recognize that right then was one of the best moments we have had in a long time.

But I want to ask what may be an embarrassing question: What have you done about it? It is not enough to define issues; we must act on them. Think of your life as a ship. You are the captain. Suddenly it comes to you that you are on a wrong course. It comes as clear as the North Star on a crisp night. And you say to yourself, "I am going to have to change my course."

Right then you give the wheel a little turn, but that is all. It is too upsetting to reverse courses or veer sharply all of a sudden. But while you delay the necessary, even the inevitable, the ship continues making headway on the wrong course. Every moment of delay takes you farther off course. It is not enough to take the readings; to analyze the problem. You have to put your hand on the wheel, and change the course.

So the strategy suggested is twofold: first, we must get out of the whirl and take a good, long, hard look at ourselves and the values we live by. If we see where things are wrong and learn that we are on the wrong course, we must act to change. In that moment, when we touch the wheel and feel the inertial forces pulling us on down the wrong course, we feel the hand of the Master, even as his hand was upon this deaf-mute, releasing new powers for new life within us.

A Clear Witness

Imagine the joy, the fulness of life, that came to this deaf-mute when he heard and spoke for the first time! A whole new world opened up to him. There were dimensions of richness and fulfilment he had never dreamed of.

Perhaps you have had such an experience in your life. It may have been a new truth of self-discovery. Or a conversion. For some it may have been the first careless rapture of a love affair.

Winston Churchill told of such an experience in his own life. It was his first attempt at painting.

Very gingerly I mixed a little blue paint on the palette with a very small brush, and then with infinite precaution made a mark about as big as a bean upon the affronted snow-white shield. It was a challenge, a deliberate challenge; but so subdued, so halting, indeed so cataleptic, that it deserved no response. At that moment the loud approaching sound of a motor-car was heard in the drive. From this chariot there stepped swiftly and lightly none other than the gifted wife of Sir John Lavery. "Painting! But what are you hesitating about? Let me have a brush—the big one."

Splash into the turpentine, wallop into the blue and white, frantic flourish on the palette—clean no longer—and then several large, fierce strokes and splashes of blue on the absolutely cowering canvas. Anyone could see that it could not hit back. No evil fate avenged the jaunty violence. The canvas grinned in helplessness before me. The spell was broken. The sickly inhibitions rolled away. I seized the largest brush and fell upon my victim with berserk fury. I have never felt any awe of a canvas since.[2]

Well now, the emancipation that is in Christ is from something far more shackling than the fear of an unmarked canvas. It is the emancipation of our true self from all the self-limiting and self-destructive claims of a passing world. Christ lifts us above our sense of guilt and shame; the defeat of our past failures. He draws together the scattered remnants of our fractured and broken purposes, and gives us a new cohesion and intensity that can turn a deaf ear to all the noises of the world. After we have been with Christ, we march to the beat of another drummer.

But the gift of speech goes with the gift of hearing. Once we have heard, we are compelled by an inner necessity to tell others. It is just too good to keep; we must share it. We must be a witness. The deaf-mute became a witness, and the worldlings around made a judgment on Jesus: " 'He has done all things well; he even makes the deaf hear and the dumb speak' " (7:37, RSV). Later on when the disciples heard and understood, they became witnesses. And we are here because a long chain of evangelized became evangelists.

Louis Evans tells of a dog that was run over by a car. A doctor hurriedly bound up its broken leg and took the dog into his own home. After weeks of care he was surprised to discover that the dog had just walked off and left him, and he had some harsh thoughts about that ungrateful dog. Two days later he heard a scratching at his front door; on the front porch he found the dog he had healed—in company with another dog that had been hurt.[3]

That is why we have this story of the deaf-mute: to remind us that we have the blessed information that must be passed on. There is one who binds up our wounds and makes us whole again.

Of all the questions that may be asked of us when we reach heaven, perhaps the most terrible would be this: "Did you tell anyone? Or did you come alone? If so, how could you?"

Notes

1. T. S. Eliot, "Choruses from the Rock," *The Complete Poems and Plays 1909-1950* (New York: Harcourt, Brace & Co., 1952), pp. 101-2.

2. Extract from "Painting As a Pastime" is reprinted with the permission of Charles Scribner's Sons from *Amid These Storms* by Winston Churchill. Copyright 1932 Charles Scribner's Sons; renewal copyright 1960 Winston S. Churchill.

3. Louis H. Evans, *Make Your Faith Work* (Westwood, N. J.: Fleming H. Revell Co., 1957), p. 158.

16 *Second Sight*
Mark 8:22-25

When God began creating, he began with light. For all the living creatures God made little windows so that the wonders of his good world could be seen in that light. God looked and saw that it was good. Man in his turn looked and agreed: the dew-fresh fruit hanging on the tree, the babbling brook on its way to the sea, the shimmering stars dancing in the velvet night sky, the lovely companion walking by his side. It was all very good, and a delight to the eye.

Sight, from the earliest moment, was a gift beyond words.

But in the Palestine of Jesus' day there were many without sight. The whole land was a dust bowl of impurities that put eyes out. Every Gospel writer tells us at least one story of a blind somebody who received sight from Jesus; Matthew and Mark tell us of two, perhaps three. The restoration of sight made a real impression on the early Christians.

John saw something more than an impressive event; he saw a symbolic significance in such a miracle. The symbolism might be put this way: Just as Jesus gave a blind man the power to see his physical world, so Jesus gives every true believer the power to see his spiritual world. This is the gift of second sight.

If the gift of physical sight was a wonder, the gift of second sight was even more wonderful. In fact, that greater wonder is woven right into the text of our miracle story here. So far as I know, this is the only miracle in which Jesus had to make a second attempt. The gift of sight did not come instantaneously.

Could it be that Mark, who is the only one to tell this story, is telling us something more, too? When we read what comes before and after the miracle, we suspect that he is.

The two chapters before the story are punctuated with the sighs of Jesus; sighs at the spiritual density of his own twelve. The miracle of the feeding of the five thousand was nothing more than a bare event to the twelve. Mark tells us: "They considered not the *miracle* of the loaves: for their heart was hardened" (Mark 6:52). A little later Jesus asks his disciples with a sigh, "Are ye so without understanding?" (7:18). And still later on: "Having eyes, see ye not?" (8:18).

In the verses immediately after the miracle before us, Jesus seeks to bring into focus just who he is and what he is doing (8:27-33). Peter expresses the hesitant surmise that Jesus is something more, but immediately afterward he protests the idea of the cross; he cannot "see" Jesus dying for the sake of the kingdom.

Now it is in the stream of this narrative we find our story. Remembering that Mark wrote this Gospel as a witness to the pagan world, it dawns on us that Mark is taking this means to confess that even the twelve had trouble "seeing" Jesus. The miracle of the blind man, whose sight is restored by degrees, seems to say that we need not be too alarmed if we have to take Christianity in small doses. Conversion—especially when from a point of view wholly alien to Christianity—may come gradually. In fact, we can expect that. Second sight comes only by degrees and by inches.

So Mark is saying something to us through this miracle, here in our own secularized, pagan society. It is something very important; something which we must take into account. I think his message might be summarized in three statements: first, each of us "sees" Jesus in a different light; second, our relationship to the Saviour, if it is vital, will grow; third, whatever else that relationship is, it must be an acceptance of Jesus as "the way, the truth, the life."

No Two Alike

When I say the word "Jesus," what comes to your mind? No doubt an image of some kind and one most probably very close to Sallman's painting of Christ. But what beyond that? Is he your hero, your ideal, your "friend in court," your ace-up-the-sleeve, your protector? What is Jesus to you? Or do you have any sharply defined image?

It is quite apparent that we are going to have to begin with this obvious fact: No two of us love exactly the same Jesus; no two of us "see" the same Saviour.

Earl Kelley tells the old Austrian folktale of the three wayfarers stopping at noon to rest beneath an oak tree. One looked up through the branches and said, "What a fine mast this oak would make for a ship such as I used to sail upon." A second, who had been a draper's assistant, said, "What a fine brown cloth my master could have dyed from this heavy bark." The third, who had spent his youth as a swineherd, said, "What fine fat pigs could be grown from the acorns which fall from this oak."

Then the author asks the question, Which of them saw the "fact" of the oak tree? And then, after citing some psychological experiments at the Hanover Institute, he makes his point: "Since the perception is the usable reality, and since no two organisms can make the same use of clues or bring the same experimental background to bear, no two of us see alike. We have no common world."[1]

This is the beginning of our problem as Christians. The external world as we see it is not the world as it is. Nor is the internal world. We are not aware of the inward darkness because we do not "see" it. Robert Short has put it well: "As natural men we wake up in life with faith in the natural and with a feeling of well-being; as men of the world we come into the world feeling that both life and we personally are basically good. It is not until we *really* wake up that we discover the precariousness of our situation."[2]

"Not until we really wake up." But are there any two of us who wake up to the same set of circumstances? In the common sense of doom which begins the Christian life there is an infinite variety of personal experiences. Jesus put it this way to Simon the Pharisee: "Her sins, which are many, are forgiven; for she loved much: but to whom little is forgiven, the same loveth little" (Luke 7:47).

So we must begin with the obvious: the image we have of Jesus will in some measure be determined by the shape of the doom which shakes us. We do not all see Jesus alike. And that means that we cannot superimpose our conversion upon someone else. Every conversion is different.

A Growing Relationship

Once we understand that Christian experiences are rooted in individual differences, and we are willing to let Christ be what he will to each of us, we come to the heart of the miracle witness. It is so simple and so obvious we might stumble right over it. And what is the witness?

Just as the blind man had a growing awareness of the external world around him through sharpening sight, just so will we have a growing awareness of Christ in the world around us through a sharpening insight. Or to put it quite directly, the reality of Christ grows on us.

This truth leads me as a minister of the Word to an intensely personal question: Is Christ growing on you with the passing of the years? Are you more involved with Christ now than a year ago? Five years ago? A decade ago?

Quite painfully a young wife found herself faced with the question of her relationship to Christ. The occasion was a visit from an old college roommate whom she had not seen for three years. In college days they both fancied themselves to be beyond the need for church and all such silliness, but since marriage Sue Wallace had made a profession and joined her husband's church. Almost immediately she had plunged into a lay visitation program, taking assignments, using tracts, arranging home prayer and Bible study sessions. Now Jill brought the whole thing to a head. Pouncing on a religious tract lying on the living room table she asked, "Do you actually read this tripe?"

"A friend left it," Sue lied, and then blushing with guilt, launched into an enthusiastic explanation of their program of visitation by the lay members, especially where there was illness, loneliness, or some other kind of need.

Sue managed to fend off her friend's patronizing air, but not without the rise of an unsettling doubt that had been taking shape for some weeks. There was a lady who had attended church for twenty years without knowing Christ, and who then had this luminous experience, only to follow up by quitting church altogether. And the married couple with whom they had a wonderful prayer session one evening, staving off another marital breakup, two days later had another quarrel, and this one broke the marriage to pieces.

Jill's questions shook Sue's faith from top to bottom. Was there anything to this thing of being a Christian? In such a strait, Sue's pastor called, asking her to visit a woman in desperate need. Her impulse was to refuse, but stifling that she wrote down the name and address. A little later, armed with a tract or two, she set out, feeling like the biggest hypocrite on earth.

Her visit took her to a woman whose needs were tremendous. There were five children, a run-down, dilapidated tenement, a mother at the end of her tether. Sue's first impulse was to think of the need for decent housing and food. What did Christ and sin and salvation have to do with this? But she braced herself.

"All have sinned," she began. Her training in sociology rose up in outrage; this was silly.

But Mrs. Thornton picked up the word.

"Sin," she said haltingly. "That's when nothing you do ever seems right. Lately I have been so sorry for the way I act. I don't want to be mean but I am. I holler at the children. Sometimes I just hate my husband because we live like this." She leaned forward, tears in her eyes. "Can Jesus help me? Is he real? Tell me what I got to do to ask him."

Sue tried to get her answer from the tract, but that would not do. Suddenly she opened her heart; told of her own emptiness, and the richness that had come. Then of her recent doubts, and how miserable she had been. And then she went on, "He's made a difference every day. Except when I wouldn't let him, except when I was ashamed of him. Even the very worst days of doubt that I've lived through have been better than the time before I knew him."

The rest of the story tells how Sue helped begin a transformation in three lives, at least: her own, Mrs. Thornton's, and Jill's, who came to see something in her friend which she wanted.[3]

The sight of the blind man came little by little. And in this quiet way, Mark is telling us that we come to see Christ in all his beauty in consequence of a growing, deepening relationship with him. Emil Ludwig, the biographer of the great, once said, "If you are to write a biography of a man, you must think with him and eat with him. You cannot make a person live in the minds of another unless you have a furious, mad, passionate relationship with him."

Perhaps our relationship with the Saviour does not begin as a "mad, passionate" devotion. But that is what it should become. The disciples started off in a kind of tentative detachment, but their attachment came to be a "mad, passionate relationship." Confirmed in their own experience was the truth and reality as it is in the Saviour, and with that confirmation caution was thrown to the winds. So with us—or, so it should be. Whatever else we say, our relationship with Jesus must be a vital, dynamic, growing reality.

> Let no man think that sudden in a minute
>   All is accomplished and the work is done—
> Though with thine earliest dawn thou shouldst begin it
>   Scarce were it ended with thy setting sun.[4]

Jesus as Way, Truth, and Life

Now we come to the essence of Mark's intent. This story is more than mere human interest, adroitly placed. Mark is writing to make the point that Jesus is not content with anything less than our "seeing" him as Saviour. The next event in the continuing narrative points this up. The disciples had a foggy notion that Jesus was something extraordinary; they went as far as to suggest that he reminded them of Elijah, John the Baptist, or some other notable person now gone from human scenes. But Jesus wanted sharper focus than that. "These were men as trees, walking." Such vague vision makes vague Christians. The whole point of the miracle is simply a dramatic way of saying that we must come to "see" Jesus as the way for us, the truth for us, and the life for us.

Decision magazine (September, 1963) reported an interview with the late C. S. Lewis, writer of *The Screwtape Letters, Surprised by Joy,* and many other works. Lewis was an unbeliever until in his middle forties. He united with the Anglican church and became a skilful apologist for Christianity in Britain. Exploring Lewis' reason for joining the church, the interviewer commented, "I believe it was Chesterton who was asked why he became a member of the church, and he replied, 'To get rid of my sins.'"

At this point Professor Lewis spoke quickly and decisively: "It is not enough to want to get rid of one's sins. We also need to believe in the one who saves us from our sins. Not only do we need to recognize that we are sinners; we need to believe in a

Saviour who takes away sin. Matthew Arnold once wrote, 'Nor does the being hungry prove that we have bread.' "

Billy Sunday perhaps said it more graphically, "Joining a church is fine, but it no more makes us a Christian to join a church than going into a garage makes us an automobile. Only the Saviour can save."

A member of Alcoholics Anonymous owned an unusually fine watch. It combined a chronometer, a stopwatch, and a few of the features of the calendar and an astronomical observatory; it indicated the days of the month, and the phases of the moon. "In fact," he said, "all it lacked was hot and cold running water."

One day the watch broke down. He knew then that he could not take it to just an ordinary jeweler; if it were to run again, he would have to send it back to the maker.

"Then one day," said this watch owner whose life had become all unstrung, "it came to me that my life was a very complicated affair, like that watch. It had broken down, and was running out of control. I decided that my only chance was to take it back to its Maker."[5]

This is precisely what Mark would have us "see"—that Jesus is more than a hero, an ideal, a friend; Jesus is the Saviour. He made us. He knows what makes us "tick." In Jesus, "God is reconciling us unto himself."

Notes

1. Earl Kelley, Marie I. Rasey, *Education and the Nature of Man* (New York: Harper & Brothers, 1952), p. 184. Used by permission of Harper & Row.

2. Robert Short, *The Gospel According to Peanuts* (Richmond: John Knox Press, 1965), p. 43.

3. Sue Wallace, "When Faith Begins to Slip Away," *Guideposts,* May, 1965, pp. 8-10.

4. F. W. H. Myers, "St. Paul," quoted in Barclay, *The Gospel of Mark,* p. 195.

5. David A. MacLennan, *Joyous Adventure* (New York: Harper & Brothers, 1952). Used by permission of publisher and author.

17 *Seeing the Glory*
Mark 9:2-13

Our Scripture passage opens on the mist-covered heights of Hermon, towering a mile and a half above the nearby Mediterranean Sea. But it is more than the setting which is mist covered; the event itself is shrouded in mystery. That we count it a miracle only attests to the unusual aspects of an intriguing and enigmatic episode.

Those involved are the Saviour and three disciples: Peter, James, and John. There is a very real sense in which the transfiguration met the needs of Jesus. On the other hand, the three disciples hid this cherished moment in their hearts that they might travel in its light on dark days that were yet to come. After the passing of a generation, three of the four Gospel writers record the transfiguration in essentially the same form. It met their needs, too, not only then, but later.

So we ascend the misty heights of Hermon once again and try to understand what it was that happened there.

Jesus and His Friends

Luke tells us that the three disciples were "heavy with sleep." Perhaps we have the dullness of the disciples to thank for the whole thing. They, like so many of us, were inclined to live with the immediate, the superficial, the obvious. Justice Oliver Wendell Holmes is reported to have remarked on one occasion, "The one-story intellect collects facts; the two-story intellect compares, reasons, and generalizes; but the three-story intellect idealizes, imagines, and predicts—with the best illumination coming through the skylight from above." It strained the disciples to keep in some semblance of order the sequence of events. They apparently had never stumbled up to the second story, except for fleeting moments, and then they immediately tumbled to the ground level where all things tend to fade one into the other.

A sentence from Joseph Conrad might well describe these friends of Jesus: "Some men go skimming over the years of existence to sink gently into a placid grave, ignorant of life to the last, without ever having been made to see all it may contain."[1] Such were these friends of Jesus. It was their dullness that made the Hermon event a necessity.

Had the disciples not been so insensitive, so imperceptive, they would surely have sensed the conflict raging in the Master's inner world. For although Jesus faced the external world with a steady gaze and a calm voice, the storm of uncertainty was already rising within.

In a study of this passage, G. Campbell Morgan looks back over the hectic events of the past weeks as given in the disciples' memoirs, and concludes that the resistance of the disciples to the announced climax of their crusade—Jesus' passion and death in Jerusalem—gave rise to some misgivings in the Saviour's heart. Jesus needed reassurance, not resistance. Jesus needed friendship, not denial.

If this be true, then the depths of the Saviour's identification with me in my humanity can only take on more profound meaning. That sentence, "He was tested in all points like as we are," means all the more.

So, because of the insensitivity of the disciples, the Father gave our Saviour what they could have given and did not—encouragement and reassurance Moses, the towering giant of Sinai, and Elijah, the bold prophet of Carmel, met our Saviour on Hermon to say, "You are on the right track, in spite of the dullness and resistance of these disciples. Go on!"

Our Saviour experienced here what every leader has known: that anguish-filled moment when, torn by self-doubt and uncertainty, he must cast the die that will give shape and form to all the future. All the great leaders of the world have spoken of such moments. Those of us who bear responsibility lesser in scope but not lesser in stress also know such pain-racked hours. Pastors and Sunday School teachers know that moment when, standing at the fork of the road, the decision must be made, the direction taken. It is comforting to me in such moments to remember that our Saviour had such a time and to recall that he has said, "I will be with you."

Jesus and His Person

The appearance of Moses and Elijah startled the heavy-lidded disciples into wondering wakefulness. For the first time the true splendor of Jesus broke through to them. They began to see the glory.

Up until now the glory had been obscured by the casual, everyday quality of their relationship. As a matter of fact, they had misread and misinterpreted most of the clues thrown out to them. Even their conclusion that Jesus was the Christ was cast in molds that could not accommodate him: they thought of some kind of political movement, with overtones of fame and fortune. Peter went as far as to say that death was the last thing he would think of for their leader! They had set themselves up to talk Jesus out of this notion about dying on a cross.

The thing that mislead them was that Jesus was so much like them they could not see the difference. He got hungry; they got hungry. He got tired; they got tired. He needed to get away from the crowds; they needed to get away from the crowds. He had need to pray; they had the same need. The only difference was a difference in degree, as far as they could tell. Now who was going to surrender everything to one of his own kind?

Ah! That was the problem: They had not yet seen the splendor, the glory. And because they had not seen Jesus for what he was they wanted to trim his demands, to tailor-make discipleship to suit themselves.

Is that not something of our trouble? The dust we have cast in our eyes obscures Jesus in his splendor. We are perfectly willing to take him as friend, as hero, as ideal—even as martyr-Saviour. But will we take him as Lord?

We want to argue the case; to trim the demands; to make Sunday a one-time affair; to edge our Christianity out from the center of life. It never dawns on us that it is his to command; it is ours to obey. We need to hear that word which the disciples heard from the hovering cloud: "This is my beloved Son; listen to him" (Mark 9:7, RSV). Is it not time that we stopped chattering about busy schedules, fatigue from the years of service rendered, desire to get off to the lake or the mountains, and listen to the Saviour? For if he is Saviour, he is also Lord. And as Lord, he commands obedience.

Appomattox, deep in the heart of Virginia, is the site of the surrender ceremony of General Robert E. Lee to General Ulysses S. Grant, after a gruelling campaign between the Union's Army of the Potomac and the South's Army of Northern Virginia. Here are depicted lifelike figures, Grant in his field fatigues, without indication of rank or distinction, Lee in his finest uniform and all the accouterments. If you have seen that confrontation, you have no doubt wondered why Grant appeared at the surrender ceremonies so casually. Why was there not more glory, more splendor? The answer is, there was glory and splendor. Beyond the "appearance" was the fact: Grant was the victor. He had brought the brilliant strategist General Lee to defeat.

And what of Lee? Why had he come in his finest? He surrendered all that he had and with the best that he had. He would not keep back a fine uniform or a special sword to parade some distant day. He surrendered all.

This pictures the meaning of misty Hermon. The disciples saw in the mist and the clouds the true glory of Jesus, God's chosen. He was to be obeyed; they were to listen to him. All this began to come clear for the first time.

Jesus and His Mission

There is one other aspect of Hermon that lies quietly here. Time is the enemy now. Few are the weeks, short are the days until these men will stand at the helm. Will the little ship flounder and run aground? Or will she sail bravely out on the uncharted seas?

Before all such questions can be answered, these men must recognize the captain, admit his authority, and commit themselves to his mission.

What is the mission of Jesus? Briefly, it is a rescue mission. Jesus himself put it this way: "The Son of man is come to seek and to save that which was lost" (Luke 19:10). In the most personal of terms, the mission of Jesus is to come to me in my estrangement, my lostness, my rebellion, and win my consent to bring me back to the Father and home. Nothing short of a death on the cross will break down my stubborn will, penetrate my obstinate rebellion. The mission of Jesus would end at a cross and an empty tomb—nothing short of that would be effective.

Jesus had accepted this fact. But his disciples must accept it, too. And the question remains, what about us? Have we accepted it? Aren't we more interested in cushions than crosses? in self-gratification than sacrifice? If not, then pray tell me how Christian people can blandly inform the nominating committee that they do not want to be obligated, that this summer they want to be free to come and go as they please?

After the death of King George V, his body was being carried through the streets of London on a gun carriage. His crown had been placed on top of the flag-covered coffin. As the cortege moved on, the cross, which is part of the symbolism of the British Crown, was jolted loose and fell to the street. One of the sailors marching behind the gun carriage picked it up, took it to the commanding officer and saluting, said, "This cross fell off, sir. It must be replaced."

The officer was a little bewildered by the untoward happening, and he asked, "Must it be replaced now?"

"Yes, sir," replied the sailor, "the crown is never complete without the cross."

We might move further into this matter and ask, What is the motive of Jesus' mission? Again, the answer can be put tersely: To meet need where it exists, as in the Saviour's story of the good Samaritan. The Jericho road runs past every life, not once a day, but many times a day. It runs down the very center of our churches. There are unmet needs all about us.

There is only one possible motive that cannot be exhausted by the burgeoning needs which meet us every day: the motive of love. This is not self-love, which is natural. It is not the love of the opposite sex, which is also the gift of nature. The love which can go on giving without exhaustion is a love that is based in another's need, not in one's own power.

Other motives have their limit. Perhaps it is revenge. There are certain things one motivated by revenge will not hesitate to do. But sooner or later, he runs out to the end—the limit—of that motivation.

Or perhaps the motive is greed. One will do much to satisfy greed, but even that motive has its limits. One may hurt, exploit, plunder, employ deceits, but at some point he stops. He says, in effect, "This far I will go, but no farther."

Perhaps one is moved by ambition. He drives, pushes, and shoves. He slaves and connives to accomplish the end his motivation designs. But there is some point beyond which motivation will not take him.

Then, he may respond to a highly honed sense of duty. He will, under the lash of this motivation, exhaust himself in services of selfless devotion. But at some point, this motive reaches its tether. There is but one motivation that has no limits. That motivation is love. Paul said, "Love never fails." If one's motivation fails before death falls, then his motive is something less than love.

How will the Saviour go about birthing such a deep-dyed motivation? These men—Peter, James, John, and the rest—were the only hope the Saviour had that his beautiful dream would not die with him on the cross. Even resurrection would count for nothing if these men were not committed, if they failed to carry the gospel.

The death of the Saviour had given these men a graphic means of understanding what love would suffer. The resurrection of Jesus assured them that love would finally triumph. And so they went forth in love.

Now the gospel, the mission of the Saviour, has passed into our hands. What are we doing with it? Are we content to chatter inanely about things that do not matter? To wander aimlessly from this to that, never giving our time and our energies to that which eternally matters?

We say that we are tired, and we are; that we need rest, and we do. But could it be that we are tired and weary because we resist? Could it be that we have never really been atop Hermon; that we have never seen the glory, either of our captain or his cause?

Notes

1. Joseph Conrad, "Typhoon," *Portable Conrad* (New York: Doubleday & Co., Inc., 1959), p. 207.

18 *Strength for Hard Going*
Mark 9:14-29

This story touches life where we live it. It follows hard on the heels of the transfiguration; it is the descent from the mountaintop to the valley. You may remember the essential details. While Peter, James, and John are with the Saviour in the luminous mountain, the nine are struggling with a stubborn and unyielding epileptic. Nothing they try seems to work. Embarrassed, frustrated, impotent—it is a desperate moment. And in that moment the Saviour comes, snatching triumph from the jaws of despair.

Later comes the inevitable question from the disciples, asked privately but poignantly: "Why could not we cast him out?" Jesus said, "This kind can come forth by nothing but by prayer and fasting." In that simple sentence is the Saviour's secret of strength for hard going.

Who of us has not known times when nothing seemed to go right? Every move, no matter how well-intentioned, turned out wrong. It may have been at work, or in the family. Or perhaps with a child, or a church task. You may be in the throes of such a moment right now. Your question, very much like the disciples, is this: "What do I do now? I have done everything I know to do except throw up my hands and quit."

To such a frame of mind this passage has a needed and vital message. It might, like ancient Gaul, be divided into three parts: first, the unconscious threat; second, the unseen presence; and finally, the unused power.

The Unconscious Threat

To understand the threat that worked on the disciples, we may profitably reconstruct this shattering experience. Earlier Jesus had given the disciples power to heal diseases and cast out devils in his name (Mark 6:7). They went out in obedience, only to discover that the power given them really worked. In one terse sentence Mark gives us a glimpse of their glowing success: "And they cast out many demons, and anointed with oil many that were sick and healed them" (6:13, RSV). It was an exciting, even exhilarating experience to see miracle after miracle take place; to break the bonds of misery; to solve the deepest problems of life for their fellowmen.

With this in the immediate past, we can enter into the mood of confidence that prevailed with the disciples as they were confronted by this father and his broken son. By now the miracle was commonplace. The disciples could not have been more confidently casual.

But what began as just another miracle soon became an awkward, humiliating, devastating debacle. The magic formula lost its power. The demon in the lad made no response at all to the words of the disciples: "In the name of Jesus, we command you to come out of him!" The only thing that happened was that the palms of the disciples' hands were cold and wet; beads of perspiration popped out on their brows; fear grabbed their hearts. It was the fear of failure.

Now, could we be honest with one another a moment and admit that this fear of failure lurks close by at all times? We refuse to accept a leadership responsibility. Why? We fear we may fail. We hold our peace when we could make a witness. Why? We fear we may fail.

> There's dignity in suffering—
> Nobility in pain—
> But failure is a salted wound
> That burns and burns again.[1]

Could we stop and ask, What is it we are called to in Christ? Success? Or are we called to faithfulness? Isaiah was called to a task which was bound to fail (Isa. 6:9-12). Our Lord's mission, humanly speaking, ended at a cross. If we can shake off the notion that we are bound to succeed; if we can sharpen the conviction that we are bound only to be faithful—then perhaps we will become more adventuresome, more open in our undertakings for the Saviour. In a speech made at Springfield, Illinois, twenty-one years before he became president of the United States, Abraham Lincoln said, "The probability we may fail in the struggle ought not deter us from the support of a cause we believe to be just."[2] That is the spirit we need.

"I asked your disciples to cast it out, and they were not able!" So they were not able. At least, they tried. That is more than some of us do. Until we are willing to risk failure that we might be faithful we have no business lifting a disdainful eyebrow at these disciples.

Do you know the story of Luther Rice? His life reads like a Horatio Alger's story in reverse. While a very young man he lost the girl he planned to marry because he committed himself to foreign mission service. When he arrived at India's door as a missionary, he was denied access (perhaps because of the War of 1812) and was eventually denied fulfilment of his dream of foreign service by developing circumstances. Returning to America to gather support for the Judsons, in whose favor he had come home, Rice organized the first Baptist Convention, which later repudiated him. Still later, he founded Columbian College—now George Washington University—only to be snubbed and forgotten by the very institution that owed its life to him. When Luther Rice died, he possessed only the clothes he wore and the books from which he preached; he was buried in a plot given by the Pine Pleasant Baptist Church of South Carolina.

But time has vindicated Luther Rice. Baptists—both North and South—recognize an incalculable debt owed. Apparent failure has become a lasting triumph. The charity his own withheld, we extend. Does this not say to us that we must shake off the haunting fear of failure, open our lives to experiment and endeavor, and be willing to fail while being faithful?

The Unseen Presence

In the story, the presence of Jesus was apparent to all. He came striding upon the scene in serene majesty, taking command of the helm at the last moment before impending disaster fell. It is thrilling just to hear the recounting of the story.

And it comes stealing over us that the story has found its way in three of the four Gospels, not for the story's sake, though it embraces all the storyteller's art. The story bore witness to a truth they desperately needed to hear. The first Gospel, Mark, comes out of the era when Peter fell a martyr; Paul was under imperial ban; the church was under persecution's fires. Like the disciples at the foot of Hermon, the disciples of the Gospel's time were driven to the wall. The pagans, like Julian the Apostate, were asking the Christians, "Now where is your carpenter?" all the while leading them to the lions and the fiery pyre. The story of the harrassed disciples spoke to them; they heard it firsthand.

Is it any different with us? True, it is not the fires of persecution that threaten us. If it were, we might be braver. But the drain of daily frustrations, irritations, demands—these threaten the vitality of our Christian lives, the quality of our faith.

Perhaps we need to ask ourselves a question that puts the issue squarely to us: Suppose by one magic wish you could do one of two things—wish all the demands made upon you away, or wish the inner strength to handle these demands with poise and serenity. Which would you wish for?

Most of us, if we understand the deeper currents of life, would wish that we had the inner strength necessary. We know that life must have a reason. Else, like Robert Frost's hired man, we have "nothing to look backward to with pride, nothing to look forward to with hope." But how do we get this inner strength?

In the story there is a remarkable exchange between the father of the epileptic and our Lord. First the father says, "If you can do anything, have pity on us and help us!"

To which Jesus replies: "If you can! All things are possible to him who believes."

And the father utters one of the most honest cries in the Bible: "Lord, I believe; help thou mine unbelief."

Now what kind of belief is it that Jesus is talking about? Is it faith in faith? Believing that the impossible is possible; it only takes a little longer?

There is a sense in which faith liberates; in which belief generates confidence and creative energy. None would deny that. We have all experienced it both positively and negatively. But the faith of which our Lord speaks lies far deeper. The Saviour was asking this distraught father to believe that underlying all things— including his smitten son—was the love of the Heavenly Father who was too good to do wrong; who was so strong he could take wrong and make it right, either in this world, or in the world to come. Jesus was asking this man to believe that the sight of his son writhing on the ground, eyes rolled back, in paroxysms and seizures, neither represented the will nor the act of God. He was asking the father to believe, "An enemy hath done this"; that with the help of the Father in heaven, the grip of the evil one could be broken.

This was asking a lot. It was asking this man to go against everything he had been taught; it was asking him to go against the evidence of his own senses. It was asking him to believe that the heartfelt interest expressed in the gentle question, "How long has he been like this?" was the true expression of God's own interest. In short, Jesus was asking this father to believe that he had found the heart of God in the compassion of the Christ before whom he stood. Studdert Kennedy asks:

> How do I know that God is good?
> I don't.
> I gamble like a man. I bet my life
> Upon one side in life's great war . .
> For God is Love. Such is my Faith, and such
> My reasons for it, and I find them strong
> Enough. And you? You want to argue?
> Well, I can't. It is a choice. I choose the Christ.[3]

This miracle must have found its way in the Gospels because it confirmed the faith of second- and third-generation Christians. They were not forsaken in the lion's reach nor on the fiery pyre. Christ was with them, and in him they found strength.

The world has seen that in our century as well as the first. An English officer, Payne Best, was a fellow prisoner with the German martyr Dietrich Bonhoeffer at Flossenberg prison. Of Bonhoeffer, the Englishman wrote in his book *The Venlo Incident:* "Bonhoeffer . . . was all humility and sweetness, he always seemed to me to diffuse an atmosphere of happiness, of joy in every smallest event in life, and of deep gratitude for the mere fact that he was alive. . . . He was one of the very few men that I have ever met to whom his God was real and close to him."

In that same book, he writes of his last glimpse of Bonhoeffer: "The following day, Sunday, April 8, 1945, Pastor Bonhoeffer held a little service and spoke to us in a manner which reached the hearts of all, finding just the right words to express the spirit of our imprisonment and the thoughts and resolutions which it had brought. He had hardly finished his last prayer when the door opened and two evil-looking men in civilian clothes came in and said: 'Prisoner Bonhoeffer, get ready to come with us.' For all prisoners those words 'come with us' had come to mean one thing only—the scaffold.

"We bade him good-bye—he drew me aside—'This is the end,' he said. 'For me the beginning of life.' . . . The next day, at Flossenberg, he was hanged."[4]

The Unused Power

Have you had the thought, "But what has all this to do with me? I am no hero, no martyr. What I need is strength to meet joyously my tasks; to stand the frustrations of my daily routine with serenity; to have power for my tasks."

Indeed. And is it not proper to observe that the difference between the martyred saint and ourselves is only one of degree? Stress is stress, no matter what its source. It is possible to become more overwrought about a detail than a true crisis. It may require as much inner serenity to live joyously in your situation as it would in a prison cell. For "iron bars do not a prison make," not always.

A preacher of another generation used to suggest that we "practice the presence of God." I know of no better way to say it. If I understand the phrase, it means to live each day simply, assuming the presence and the power of God in each moment: sustaining, strengthening, underlying all of life. The renowned Spurgeon used to say, "A little faith will bring your soul to heaven, but a great faith will bring heaven to your soul."

During and immediately after World War I, Walter Rauschenbush labored in one of the desperately blighted areas of New York City, called Hell's Kitchen. It was a work that never let up; a work in which the demands made were more than any person could possibly hope to meet. And out of those days, days of surpassing strain, Rauschenbush wrote:

In the castle of my soul
Is a little postern gate,
Whereat, when I enter,
I am in the presence of God.
In a moment, in the turning of a thought,
I am where God is.
This is a fact.

When I enter into God,
All life has a meaning,
Without asking I know;
My desires are even now fulfilled,
My fever is gone
In the great quiet of God.
My troubles are but pebbles on the road,
My joys are like the everlasting hills.

So it is when my soul steps through the postern gate
Into the presence of God.
Big things become small, and small things become great.
The near becomes far, and the future is near.
The lowly and despised is shot through with glory . . .
God is the substance of all revolutions;
When I am in Him, I am in the Kingdom of God.
And in the Fatherland of my Soul.[5]

Shining through those lines is evidence that there is strength for hard going. It is there for us. We must discipline ourselves; humble ourselves; become enough like a child to ask for it and receive it.

Notes

1. Margery Howell, "Wormwood," as cited in Stevenson, *The Home Book of Quotations* (New York: Dodd, Mead & Co., 1964), p. 612.
2. Cited in *ibid.*, p. 11.
3. G. Studdert Kennedy, "Faith," in *The Unutterable Beauty*, pp. 101-4.
4. Dietrich Bonhoeffer, *Letters and Papers from Prison* (London: Fontana Books, 1959), p. 11.
5. Walter Rauschenbush, "The Little Gate to God," in *Masterpieces of Religious Verse*, p. 72.

19 From Rags to Riches
Mark 10:46-52

There is a gap between the miracle at the foot of Hermon and the miracle on the edge of Jericho. That gap is filled with narrative that moves at breathtaking pace. As we are carried along with the story it occurs to us that this is not all of it, only the gist of it. It is told in dots and dashes, and in condensed form.

It is interesting reading: conversations of Jesus with his disciples, his friends, his enemies, his would-be followers. One scene flows into the next with a relentless urgency. To know the grinding climax toward which the story moves is to experience an urge to slow the whole thing down; to fill out more of the small details; to postpone the inevitable. But that is not the purpose: simply to tell a story. The purpose is to declare a gospel. All that is irrelevant is stripped away.

Perhaps that is why Mark omits the dramatic conversion of Zacchaeus, which also happened in Jericho (Luke 19:1-10). Or it may be that Mark did not have the Zacchaeus story in his material. Whatever the reason for the omission, we do have the story of Bartimaeus, and his recovery of sight.

There is a bit of the gospel in this miracle, else it would not be here. Three truths slip quietly out of the story into my own heart: first, ragged beggars; second, the seeking brother; third, the transformation—from rags to riches.

Ragged Beggars

The northern gate of Jericho was the haunt of this miserable beggar Bartimaeus. We can only dimly imagine the bleak existence that made up the dreary round of his days and nights. The Palestine in the days of Jesus offered a life which at best was hard; at worst, it was well-nigh impossible. Bartimaeus had life at its worst. The sum of his life was little more than a cipher.

The fact that he was a beggar is the ground of his identity

with today's moderns. Bartimaeus was a beggar in rags; we are beggars in velvet.

> Hark, hark, the dogs do bark,
> The beggars are coming to town,
> Some in rags, some in tags,
> And some in velvet gowns.

Whether in rags or in velvet, all are beggars. That we are is not immediately apparent. In fact, the external evidence runs in the other direction. Not long ago the *Wall Street Journal* reported some interesting facts about automobile distribution among the industrialized nations of the world. One Englishman in twelve owns a car; in prosperous Switzerland, it is one in thirteen. In West Germany it is one in sixteen, and in Italy, one in thirty-four. But here in America, one in three own cars. If we are beggars, we are beggars on wheels.

We are also beggars with money in our jeans as well. At the end of 1963, the U.S. Bureau of Labor Statistics' "Market Basket" (the wage necessary to maintain a typical wage earner's standard of living, including an automobile and a TV) was set at $4,955. But the median income of American families was $5,200 per family, *after taxes.* However, the real significance of the American distribution of wealth lies not in this $250 per year surplus of the median figure; it lies with those families which enjoy an even greater surplus. With eight million U.S. families (involving more than twenty-seven million people) enjoying after-tax incomes of $10,000 or more, it appears that many Americans are beginning to approach the level of real privilege. Reliable predictions indicate this privileged class in America may increase by another ten million long before the year 1970.[1]

We have more to live with and less to live for. We can do more things, go more places, enjoy more privileges than ever before; yet life is emptier than ever before. What are we doing with this excess wealth? Wealth carries with it responsibility.

A recent release from the Baptist Press states that church attendance in America increased by 30 percent during the last decade. Total church membership is now 118 million. Yet illegitimacy has increased ten times faster than church membership growth. Venereal disease has increased 72 percent during the past year. Crime is increasing four times faster than the population. There are now seven million alcoholics in the nation. There are 175,000 more taverns than the combined total of all churches, synagogues, and temples. The American people gamble away more money each year than they spend on religion, medicine, education, and automobiles.

In commenting on this sad compilation of statistics, E. S. James editorialized:

The most tragic fact in the statistics is that a vast number of these who have departed so far from the straight path were once regular in attendance at church, and many of them are still present most [sic] every Sunday. It is good that they have attended services and do, but something is dreadfully wrong when people can sit under the influence of the church's ministry and go right out to seek new ways to sin.[2]

Claire Cox of the United Press in *The New Time Religion* gives a detailed description of modern American religion with the words: "There is a new-time religion in the land. It has made the church more popular and prosperous than ever before. It has also made the church less pious." Franklin Littell, professor of church history and an authority in his field, wrote recently in a professional magazine: "(With) the 'new Christians' in America, the morning star of the Great Century of Christian Missions, the problems are like those on the other mission fields; to begin to make out of remarkable statistical gains something qualitatively worthy of the name 'Christian.' "[3]

And in this national foment, all of us are caught up. We are double-minded most of the time, feeling a pull toward honest discipleship, and also feeling a drag toward the gaudy midway of a tinselled and tantalizing world. We know what Jesus meant about the house divided: we live in it. We identify with the two women friends who happened to meet at the door of their psychiatrist's office. "Hello," said one. "Are you coming or going?" "If I knew that," replied the other, "I wouldn't be here."

The irony of the passage then is that our identity is with the poor beggar, Bartimaeus. He was a beggar in rags; we are beggars in velvet.

The Seeking Brother

We do not live very long before we learn for ourselves that there are some things that money cannot buy: peace of mind, a sense of belonging, a conviction of meaning. Life involves all the fundamental mysteries; there is always a loose end flailing us. Some time ago in the *New Yorker* there appeared a seventy-seven word short story. A lad in Summit, New Jersey—just six years old—who had recently learned to count, asked his mother what was the last, last, very last number countable. The mother answered that he could count, and count, and count, but he could never, never count that last number. She turned away thinking how neatly she had slipped the concept of infinity into her son's mind, but when she turned back to him, he was lying on his bed softly weeping.[4]

He wanted life to be neater than that. Don't we all?

But what has this to do with blind Bartimaeus? Simply this: like the blind beggar or the six-year-old counter, as beggars in velvet we sooner or later discover that life is bigger than we are; that if we ever get to that "last number" we are going to have to have help.

In our darkness—even as Bartimaeus in his—we peer out anxiously for some ray of light; some glimmer of hope. And like Bartimaeus, we hear of Jesus. It may have been as a child; it may have been of late. But we have heard of Jesus. And we hear that Jesus is God, come in human form, to be what we are that he might bring us to what he is. And like Bartimaeus, hardly knowing what we do, we call out, "Jesus . . . have mercy on me!"

But who is this Jesus? Is he some kind of ace-in-the-hole we keep for extraordinary crises? Is he a kind of religious rabbit's foot you keep handy for good luck? Or is he God—as he claims?

Our question is very much like the question put to me this past week as I rode my bicycle home from an errand. Two preschoolers were playing in their sandpile and looked up to see me—a grown man—riding by. "Hey!" they cried. "Are you a brother?" It was a question about identity.

"Are you our brother?" That is the question we ask of Jesus.

"For if you are our brother, then your Father is our Father; and that is a comfort."

Emmanuel Kant, the German philosopher, once wrote: "It is at once an absurd and presumptuous delusion to try by persistent importunity of prayer (to see) whether God might not be deflected from the path of his wisdom to provide some momentary advantage for us." For Kant, that was a logical deduction. For him, God was sovereign law in the physical universe and in man's conscience—a law that was not to be swayed by any personal concerns. But Jesus comes, calling God not "law" but Father, and that is a new dimension altogether.

Yes. If Jesus is my brother, then God is my Father, too. And I can move calmly with numbers I can't count and mysteries I can't fathom, because at the heart of it all is a loving Father.

From Rags to Riches

Earlier we raised the question of the gospel that lies in this miracle. What is it? Alan Richardson states the meaning of this miracle to the infant church in words that are concise and almost poetical:

Men sit helpless in blindness and poverty until Jesus draws near and they learn to call upon Him. Despite the hindering clamour of the world, they can, if they have faith, hear the voice of Jesus calling to them. When they rise in obedience to His call, they are saved ("made whole") from their blindness and poverty, and must now begin at once to "follow Jesus in the way" of discipleship. The faith of which this miracle-story speaks, the faith of blind Bartimaeus, is not faith in a healer (in the secular sense of "faith-healing"); it is rather *Christian* faith, or *saving* faith.[5]

That was the meaning of this story to Mark and his contemporaries when he first set down his Gospel. It is also the meaning for many of us. We may state it differently, according to our own experience; the meaning is the same: we have come from spiritual rags to spiritual riches, by faith in Jesus Christ.

This past spring a lovely young woman made a profession of faith in one of a series of evangelistic services I was conducting. It was not a spur-of-the-moment decision; it was the end of a long quest. She had come from an entirely different religious background. She had known religion; she had never known the Saviour. But now she did, and her public commitment to Christ one night during that meeting followed. Her parents opposed her openly; the decision was difficult. Two days later she wrote the pastor a letter. It put into a contemporary setting the miracle of which Bartimaeus' story is a symbol:

Dear Pastor:
I can't begin to describe the feeling that I have. It is one of supreme happiness and joy. I have come to know the Lord and I realize how fortunate I am. I profess my faith with untold joy. This has been a complete and horrible struggle; but now my struggle is over and my life beginning. I hope to participate in the church activities as much as possible. Through my faith I hope to bring my parents to know the Lord. I find it difficult now to make myself understood but I know the Lord will help me. Between the two of us I have great hopes for my family. I do not blame them. I pray for them.
Thank you for your guidance and faith and may you continue always to preach God's Word.

A modern beggar-in-velvet who came to Christ and in the coming experienced the joy of exchanging her spiritual rags for Christ's true riches.

Notes

1. Material drawn from *Life Magazine*, editorial, volume 54, no. 1. January 4, 1963.

2. E. S. James, *Baptist Standard*, September 30, 1964.

3. Franklin H. Littell, *Church Management*, March, 1965, p. 9.

4. Carlyle Marney, *Dangerous Fathers, Problem Mothers, and Terrible Teens* (Nashville: Abingdon Press, 1958), p. 25.

5. Richardson, *op. cit.*, p. 89.

20 A Dark Miracle

Mark 11:12-14,20-26

The only dark miracle Jesus ever worked occurred early one Monday morning in the last week of his life. It was the morning after the Palm Sunday reception Jerusalem gave him. Jesus had taken refuge from the tumult and the crowds in the home of his dear friends Mary, Martha, and Lazarus in suburban Bethany.

Early Jesus began the walk with his disciples back into the city. Now walking generates hunger, and our Saviour was no exception. The sight of a fig tree in full leaf held hope of nourishment, though the season for such was still in prospect. (Fig trees in Palestine usually produce fruit in June, and this was earlier. The leaves come out after the fruit: a kind of advertising.) Jesus went to the tree in full foliage, but there was nothing. The tree was lying with its leaves. Unexpectedly, Jesus said, loud enough for the disciples to hear, "May no one ever again eat fruit from you!"

When the disciples came by that night it was too dark to see what had happened. But the next morning, when they came to the tree, Peter remembered, and Peter looked. The leaves were brown; the tree was drying up. It startled even Peter: "Master, look! The fig tree you cursed has withered."

The chill thought comes creeping over us that such petulance is out of character for our Saviour. True, the noncanonical literature abounds with such dark miracles, but none of them was judged authentic: the canon was barred to them. Only this one is authentic. Matthew and Mark agree to that, although Luke is silent. Some tidy scholars, troubled by the dark side of the cursing miracle, have tried to explain it away. But here it is as Mark tells it, and Matthew agrees that it happened.

What Christ Cursed

What was it the Saviour cursed? Was it something more than a false tree? Say, a false pretension? The miracle story is divided into two parts. Between the cursing and the confirmation Mark has inserted another story. In this quiet way, Mark is casting a bit of light on this dark miracle.

So we read on and before we are ten words past the cursing incident we are immersed in one of the most dramatic moments in all the life of the Saviour. We are in the Temple, in the midst of the whole slick business of fleecing the poor, exploiting the innocent. Here is the Jewish religion at its highest moment (the week of the Passover) and at its lowest morality (the Passover sacrifice trafficking and trading). The house of prayer has been converted to a livestock market, and the stench is stifling.

The vendors hark their wares: a lamb for the wealthy; a dove for the poor. They have a monopoly—the inspectors see to that. Necessity and convenience drive the prices up, and the price is paid in the Temple coinage—another neat little racket. No coins within the Temple have the value of a Temple coin, and the priests and their henchmen pocket the percentage. Neither are the inspectors innocent. Even the Temple stamp is not enough; the bribe must be right, too. From beginning to end, from first to last, it is a fleecing operation.

What brings these people to accept and impose such indignities? It is not so much innocence as venality. It is blackmail in both directions. Why don't they protest? Some did, to be sure. John was one who had a following. But what of the rest? The whole business of forgiveness, salvation, acceptance with God is put on the basis of a conniving deal, with both parties reeking with guilt.

And "these are the people of God"; they are to sire the Christ; to "let judgment roll as the waters, and righteousness as a mighty stream." These are they through whom "all the families of the earth are to be blest" (Amos 5:24; Gen. 12:3). They knew all the proof texts; they could recite all the messianic promises. They knew the written Word; they did not know the incarnate Word when he came into their midst. Some had a vague suspicion, but they knew if it were true it would completely dislocate this religious gimmick they all had going for them.

So when Christ walked in that Monday morning, they were all so busy incriminating one another with their traffic of expiation, salvation, and eternal life that they did not even notice him. Not until the fireworks started. The whole stinking business sent Jesus into an active fury, and when he got through, the place was a real shambles. The vendors and the priests were salvaging the pieces and licking their wounds.

Later on, the disciples understood about the tree. Jesus would not send his withering blast upon men and destroy them, he would do that on an unfeeling tree. But blast he would that they might understand that he would never have patience with pretense or fraud, no matter how pious.

Are our own spiritual postures tinged, however slightly, with fraud? Ask yourself the question: Am I absolutely honest in my religious life? The repentance of a hypocrite can be the greatest hypocrisy. How can we avoid this plague Jesus so dramatically condemned? Perhaps a personal experience will show the way.

It was the final meeting of a denominational committee. What several had suspected, investigation had confirmed. One of the five members of our small committee had been using his position to further his own ends and, in the process, had practiced a deceit clothed in piety. I am not yet convinced the member knew his own fraud; he had fabricated a rationalization.

On the morning of May 9 we were convened for a final session. One of our members, a former congressman, asked the chairman for the floor on personal privilege. In the moments that followed, the former congressman (calling the fraudulent member by name) said something like this:

The New Testament says, "If a brother be overtaken in a fault, you that are spiritual restore such an one, in the spirit of meekness, considering thyself, lest thou also be tempted." It is difficult for me, a layman, to be speaking thus to a member of the clergy. However, I feel that you have been something less than honest with us.

Perhaps we are at fault in this. I must confess that I have not wholly trusted you in this matter. Further, I have been suspicious that you might be serving other ends than the work of this committee. For this suspicion I want to apologize. From now on I shall trust you.

Back in 1951, while serving in the United States Congress, I found myself sitting on committees of that body examining witnesses. We were attempting to discover the truth in certain areas that would affect the legislation before the entire body. It was a difficult assignment.

While sitting thus on a congressional committee, I was reminded by a series of events—and particularly a sermon—that I had not always been wholly honest. I had been less than honest with my wife, on occasion. I had been less than honest with my son. Painfully I came to admit that I had some changes to make, and I set about in an effort to be as scrupulously honest with all men—and with the members of my own family—as God gave me power to know honesty and do it.

Within the next few days I sat down and wrote a letter to my son, asking his pardon. I told him that I had not been wholly honest with him, and this letter was my pledge that I would be so in the future.

I wrote a similar letter to my wife.

On the following Easter I went home for a few days' vacation. It was one of the finest periods in my life. My son opened up to me in a way that was almost embarrassing. I came to realize how much my little dishonesties had shut out of my life. For the first time I knew the full joys of being a father to my own son.

Since then I have tried to keep that vow. In all my dealings with my fellowmen I have tried to be completely honest and aboveboard. It is the only way.

The Saviour taught that we must seek to live in such transparent sincerity that whatever gap exists between intent and deed will be the failure of mind and not of heart. And such failure, the grace extended us in Christ will cover. Anything less, he rejects.

What Christ Taught

The lesson Christ taught the disciples when they took note of the miraculous blight is couched in one brief sentence: "Have faith in God." Before the week was out, they would need faith like that. Jesus knew the coming events might likely blot God out of their reckoning.

Trouble has a way of making God fade out. In a way, trouble is like fog. The Bureau of Standards in Washington made a study and discovered that a fog one hundred feet high, covering seven city blocks, and dense enough to blot out vast buildings, the sky,

and even the sun was composed of sixty thousand million drop-
lets of water. But if you were to wring all that water out of
the atmosphere, making the fog disappear and all the imposing
realities of the city reappear, you would have about enough water
to fill one drinking glass.

When trouble comes into our lives it has a way of obscuring
the abiding realities by which we must live. Perhaps the escaped
prisoners who hid in a cellar of Cologne during World War II did
not know how trouble will hide the face of God. But a passing
prisoner took the time and the trouble to inscribe on the wall
his own credo: "I believe in the sun, even when it is not shining. I believe in love, even when feeling it not. I believe in
God, even when He is silent."

"Have faith in God," said Jesus to the twelve. He may have
been thinking of that black Friday through which they would pass
before the Easter sunrise. They would need to have faith; there was
plenty to instil a fear. They had been walking in day, but the
night was about to fall. Would their faith sustain them then? In
the crypt of Allegheny Observatory at the University of Pittsburgh
there is an inscription which reads: "We have loved the stars too
fondly to be fearful of the night." Would the twelve see the
twinkling stars when the night fell? Jesus took this means of
reminding them that if we look with the eyes of faith, then the
darker the night, the brighter the stars.

The night was rapidly falling. While the disciples marvelled at
the word which had withered the fig tree, Jesus said simply, "Have
faith in God." It was a word they needed.

What Christ Encouraged

We sometimes talk about "faith that moves mountains," as
though faith could do it alone. But Jesus talked about having
faith in a *God* who can move mountains. And the Saviour encouraged his friends to pray to a God like that, and to believe
they would be heard.

Why are we so surprised when our prayers are answered? Is
it that we have so little real faith in them?

> So joyously, at answered prayer,
> The heart leaps up from its despair—

> It must indeed have been afraid
> God wasn't listening when it prayed.[1]

Perhaps it is experience which teaches us to use caution in our prayers: to hedge them in; to make them tentative. We have prayed, but if there was an answer, it seemed to us to be an answer turned wrong side out. Is this what has taken the confidence out of our praying?

Perhaps we need to look further. It just could be that the answer which seemed to be a no instead of a yes was in our own best interest. Perhaps an experience from the life of Bertha Smith, who served as missionary in China and Formosa for forty-one years, will cast a light on this.

It was the morning of January 11, 1937. The Japanese were bombing Tsining; the foot soldiers were poised to overrun the prostrate city. Of that morning, Miss Smith writes:

I had spiritual sense enough to know that the only way to be acceptable in God's holy presence was by identifying myself with Christ in his death. Because I was doing this I knew that the mighty Creator, the sustainer of the universe, was listening to me. I prayed, "Lord, there come those instruments of torture flying out of the pit of hell! [I did not mean from Japan—I meant from the devil himself.] Now, for the sake of these helpless people who have no way of escape, will you take charge of those planes! Hold the hands of the bombardiers and do not let those bombs fall anywhere on this city today except where you permit them to fall."

It seems to me that Miss Smith, although she did not say so specifically, had her own mission compound in mind. But a little after eleven that same morning two bombs fell—one in the yard of the compound, the other nearby—and the two-story brick building where Miss Smith did her work and lived was a shambles. She had to take shelter with the Presbyterian mission. Her Chinese co-workers asked, "Why did God, in whom we were trusting, permit those bombs to drop here on our mission grounds?"

All she could say was, "This is not evil. The Lord permitted this for some purpose. He, the mighty God, does not have to explain himself to human beings—at least not now."

Well, the city fell to the Japanese after fierce ground fighting. Two days later Miss Smith went back to the compound with Japanese officers to file a claim for damages from the bombing. But the damage they saw was from more than bombing. The compound was riddled from the shelling of mortars. Two shells had entered Miss Smith's quarters. The iron bed was blasted. Round bullets the size of a thumb were scattered all over the floor. Parts of twenty shells, exploded and unexploded, were found in the building and on the grounds. The commanding officer said something to the interpreter, who flipping valiantly from page to page in his Japanese-to-English dictionary, finally came up with the translation: "I . . . ad-mit . . . it . . . is . . . a . . . des-per-ate . . . sit-u-a-tion!" Miss Smith finished her story with this observation.

While I quite agreed with him that it was a desperate situation, I was thrilling over the fact that the mighty God hears our prayers. He had guided the hands of those pilots and allowed those bombs to be dropped into our mission grounds in order to scatter us all out from there, that perhaps he might save the lives of some and protect the nerves of all.[2]

The disciples marvelled at the withered fig tree. Jesus said, in effect: "That is nothing, nothing at all. We have a great and good Heavenly Father—too good to do wrong. Pray to him in faith. He will hear. He will answer. It may not be the gift you want; it will be the gift you need.

I asked God for strength that I might achieve,
I was made weak that I might learn humbly to obey . . .
I asked for health that I might do great things,
I was given infirmity that I might do better things . . .
I asked for riches that I might be happy,
I was given poverty that I might be wise . . .
I asked for power that I might have the praise of men,
I was given weakness that I might feel the need of God . . .
I asked for all things that I might enjoy life,
I was given life, that I might enjoy all things . . .
I got nothing that I asked for—but everything I had hoped for;
Almost despite myself my unspoken prayers were answered.
I am among all men most richly blest.[3]

What did Jesus curse? Pretense. What lesson did the Saviour teach? Faith in God. What did our Lord encourage? Confident prayer. That is the witness of the miracle of the blasted fig tree.

Notes

1. Elaine V. Emans, "The Surprise," quoted in Tennessee Baptist Convention mail-out *Quotes and Facts*.

2. Bertha Smith, *Go Home and Tell* (Nashville: Broadman Press, 1965), pp. 85-89.

3. Glenora Lincoln, from Abilities, Inc.

21 *The Death of Death*

Mark 16:1-5

As we cast a backward glance across the way we have come, it seems we have traveled a soaring arch that bridges two worlds: the temporal and the eternal; the finite and the infinite; God's and man's. And now we are nearer that other world where God dwells than at any time in our journey. We stand on the threshold of the resurrection event—the greatest miracle of them all.

Although this mightiest of all the wonders done by Jesus comes at the end of the story, we sense that we are in the presence of something more than the climax of the story. It is more like the keystone of the arch: without this miracle the rest would be nothing but curiosity pieces. It is the resurrection event which gives everything else authenticity. All else rests on this—even the miracle in our own hearts. This is the miracle that makes all the others credible.

Here is the miracle that speaks most directly to our own need. It is the Christian answer to man's mysterious end: the mystery of death. Death is that dark malady which casts its shadow over the bright joys of life. Death stalks us; he haunts our dreams; his power holds us. Not many of us would call death a friend. To be sure, when the fog swirls in, and the mists of pain descend, we may call him friend. But if death becomes friendly, it is because life has become bitter. Death may not terrify us, but we don't want him for everyday company either. He is still the enemy.

One of the many reasons this is true may be that we know so little about death. "It is the undiscovered country from whose bourne no traveler has e'er returned." We fear what we do not know, and no man knows death firsthand.

Thomas Wolfe came as close as anybody. In a letter to his old friend Maxwell Perkins, chief editor of Charles Scribner's Sons, Wolfe tells us how he felt when he could feel death breathing down his neck. Following is the letter which was written from

Providence Hospital, Seattle, Washington, just two days before his death:

DEAR MAX:

I'm sneaking this against orders, but "I've got a hunch" and I wanted to write these words to you.

I've made a long voyage and been to a strange country, and I've seen the dark man very close; and I don't think I was too much afraid of him, but so much of mortality clings to me—I wanted most desperately to live and still do, and I thought about you all a thousand times, and wanted to see you all again, and there was the impossible anguish and regret of all the work I had not done, and of all the work I had to do—and I know I'm just a grain of dust and I feel as if a great window had been opened on life I did not know about before—and if I come through this, I hope to God I am a better man, and in some strange way I can't explain I know I am a deeper and a wiser one. If I get on my feet and out of here, it will be months before I head back, but if I get on my feet, I'll come back.

Whatever happens—I had this "hunch" and wanted to write you.[1]

Wolfe expresses a feeling we have all known. Death is an enemy. We cannot evade him: this ambiguous life, no matter where it goes or what it does, always ends at the grave.

The grave. That is the link between us and Jesus. His beautiful life came to a sad and apparent end at the grave. It is his grave that makes us know he is our brother. But what happened *in* that grave makes us know that he is our Saviour. Death died in that grave; hope was born there. So here is the last and best miracle, the resurrection event, without which none of the other miracles would really matter.

So that we can move with a sense of direction, let me suggest an order to help us think through the resurrection: first, the conquest of death; then, the creation of faith; and finally, the continuing life.

The Conquest of Death

Mark is a bit scant in his telling of the event. So we turn to Matthew for the beginnings of this strange sequel to Good Friday. There is a clue in the uneasy premonition of the religious leaders:

Now the next day, that followed the day of the preparation, the chief priests and Pharisees came together unto Pilate, saying, Sir, we remember that that deceiver said, while he was yet alive, After three days I will rise again. Command therefore that the sepulchre be made sure until the third day, lest his disciples come by night, and steal him away, and say unto the people, He is risen from the dead: so the last error shall be worse than the first. Pilate said unto them, Ye have a watch: go your way, make it as sure as ye can (Matt. 27:62-65).

Death had Jesus in his icy grip; a secure guard was set at the opening of the grave; a great stone was rolled against the opening of the tomb. Death and fear have done their worst, but neither death nor fear could hold the vital energy loosed within the cave-tomb. God has entered the lists. He who spoke the worlds into being grapples with death, and death has met his match.

What can boulders, or poor soldiers, yea death himself do? Jesus Christ, our brother, made death die!

In his book on eastern travel, titled *Eothen*, A. W. Kinglake tells of a night on the desert when they pitched their tents in the sand with no sign of inhabited land. But that night an Arab stalked out of the camp across the sands. He returned in the morning with a fresh green blade of rice. In the desolation of our land of sin and death, Jesus slips out in the dark night to bring back the fresh green of life eternal. Here is no accident, no inexplicable exception to the normal process of human existence, but an act of God. Death took hold of the manhood of Jesus and slew him; God took hold of the death in Jesus, and death died.

Christ is become the firstfruits of them that sleep.

> Seek ye the Lord?
> Search not the cold and empty tomb;
> He is not linked with night and gloom;
> He is not bound by death and strife;
> His name is Light and Love and Life!
> He lives! Is risen! Go find ye then
> The living Lord—in the hearts of men!
>
> M. Ethel Anderson

The Creation of Faith

The resurrection is the keystone in the disciples' arch of faith. Read the New Testament accounts again, and you are struck with the transformation the resurrection event made in the disciples. That which had been only a tentative conclusion became a fixed conviction. Thomas, who was the last to surrender his arms, cried out, "My Lord, and my God!" This cry was the summary of each man's faith.

Al Capp, creator of Li'l Abner and Daisy Mae, has created a technique for the entertainment of large audiences with his drawing pencil. Using a projection machine that carries his sketching to a screen fifty feet away, Mr. Capp draws each character in such a way that the audience is in the dark as to its identity until he stops and says, "This is the line that makes the difference." With a quick stroke of the pencil the line is added and all present recognize the character the artist has been drawing.

The resurrection event was the "line that made the difference." The glorified body of Jesus was both familiar and unfamiliar. They could recognize Jesus—his voice, his hands, his features. But they could not limit Jesus. Neither time nor place bound him. He appeared through closed doors. Now he was in Jerusalem, or was it the road to Emmaus, or was it Galilee?

When the disciples stood to preach a few weeks later in Jerusalem, the resurrection event was the keystone of their faith:

Ye men of Israel, hear these words; Jesus of Nazareth, a man approved of God among you by miracles and wonders and signs, which God did by him in the midst of you, as ye yourselves also know: him, being delivered by the determinate counsel and foreknowledge of God, ye have taken, and by wicked hands have crucified and slain: whom God hath raised up, having loosed the pains of death: because it was not possible that he should be holden of it. This Jesus hath God raised up, whereof we all are witnesses (Acts 2:22-24,32).

Lazarus had been raised from the dead in Bethany, but only to die again. He was still a man, bound by the limits of time and space. But in Jesus the resurrection event was the line "that made the difference." His resurrection was of a different order. The resurrection life of Christ was both familiar and unfamiliar, known and unknown. It was God's new dimension. The resurrection created faith.

It is the resurrection of Jesus which we celebrate at Easter that makes the difference for the Christian, too. This is our evidence that death is not the final word: "Now is Christ risen from the dead, and become the firstfruits of them that slept" (1 Cor. 15:20). Paul wrote, "I would not have you to be ignorant, brethren, concerning them which are asleep, that ye sorrow not, even as others which have no hope" (1 Thess. 4:13). The pagans are filled with anxiety and dread at the thought of death. But they know of no resurrection! The resurrection event is more than a mere worldview, such as that the earth is a sphere; that Columbus discovered America; that George Washington is the father of our country. The resurrection event is a fact of world history; if we are Christian, it is a fact of our own personal history as well.

A young man of skeptical mind was walking through the cemetery on a late fall afternoon. His spirit was overcome with heaviness as he thought of these who once had lived, worked, hoped, and dreamed. But all had ended at the grave. It was an oppressive thought. He reached in his pocket, took out a card, and wrote down his somber thoughts:

> To think of summers yet to come,
>   Of days that are to be;
> To think of weeds that are to bloom
>   Of dust that once was me!

He put the card in the bark of an old oak tree, and went on.

The next day a lovely Christian girl came to that cemetery to place flowers on the grave of her mother and father. She was alone in the world, except for the living Christ in her heart. And as she walked along, her eye happened to catch the white card in the tree. She went over, took the card down, and read it. It certainly did not express her outlook. Turning the card over, she added a second verse to the little poem:

> To think when heaven and earth have fled,
>   And time and seasons' o'er;
> And all that can die shall be dead,
>   Then I shall die no more!

The resurrection creates faith. It takes the sting from death.

The Continuing Life

The resurrection event makes death a transition, not a boundary. Eternal life begins now, and death is nothing more than a milestone.

> Death is a dialogue between
>   The spirit and the dust.
> "Dissolve," says Death; the spirit, "Sir,
>   I have another trust."
> Death doubts it, argues from the ground.
>   The spirit turns away,
> Just laying off, for evidence,
>   An overcoat of clay.[2]

How is this done? William Law once said, "The whole of the gospel is this: the birth of the holy Christ within us, so that his conquering life overcomes our inward death."

Here is a hope that rests not upon wish thoughts, nor illusions, nor even logic but upon a twofold fact: the risen Christ of history and the living Christ within. The mystic screen between the unseen and the seen fades away, and we literally live with "one foot in heaven."

If heaven is not real, it is because we have not let it be. The resurrection event is given that it might be. Grace Nies Fletcher in her book *In My Father's House* tells of her minister father in New England a generation ago. One afternoon the doorbell rang and the parson, whom everybody called by his first name, answered. It was Molly Stark. "Lee, I've got to talk with you," she said. "I'm going to die."

"Well, we all are, Molly," Lee replied. "Come in and sit down and relax." So Lee talked with her calmly as she collected herself. The doctor had just told her she had about four months left, if she were lucky.

After a while she said, "Lee, you're wonderful. But you see, I don't mind so much for myself: it's Jimmy. I can't leave Jimmy." He was her ten-year-old son who sang in the Junior choir. "He's so young," she continued. "His father's a good man, but has never quite grown up. I'm worried."

Lee didn't answer immediately. His thoughts returned to his own little son, Bildad, who had died as an infant about five years previously.

Finally he said, "Molly, I'll make a bargain with you. I'll look after your Jimmy if you'll ride herd on my Bildad. He must be about five by now . . . the right age for kindergarten down here. So you see him, and tell him his pop said that you were to look after him. And when he goes to school if he gets any D's on his report card, you can give him what for!"

Molly was laughing and crying at the same time. "Lee, it is a bargain. You make it seem so . . . so everyday. Funny, everyone has to die, but you never expect it to happen to you."

Then Lee's voice was soft as he said, "What people forget, Molly, is that we're living in eternity right now. The Lord holds the past, the present, and the future—and all families, wherever they are—together, safe in his hands. When you believe that, you can go on."[3]

"Death, be not proud!" cried old John Donne. "Death, you too shall die." He was right. Death has lost his sting now, and one day he shall lose his hold: "Then death and the underworld were hurled into the fiery lake. This is the second death—the fiery lake. If anyone's name was not found written in the book of life, he was hurled into the fiery lake" (Rev. 20:14-15, Williams). The resurrection miracle is the promise, the forecast, of the death of death for every man in Christ. But more, it is that miracle which makes all the other miracles credible; that makes Jesus' Word a word of hope that does not pass away.

Notes

1. A copy of this letter was given the author from the private library of George Edward Wallace, Knoxville, Tennessee.

2. Emily Dickinson, "Death," in *1000 Quotable Poems* (New York: Willett, Clark & Co., 1937), p. 318.

3. Grace Nies Fletcher, *In My Father's House* (New York: McGraw-Hill Book Co., Inc., 1955).

Debit

To all
my teachers
"A light shone from the mind of you"

It was the summer of 1964 in Louisville, Kentucky. I was listening, along with others, to a lecture on the Gospel of Mark. The lecturer was Professor William Hull of our Baptist seminary there. Somewhere along the way the young professor pointed out the obvious intimations in the New Testament that each Gospel writer had to be selective in his use of material about our Saviour. None could use all of it; each used that which was adaptable to his purpose. The technical name for this fact was given: *redactiongeschichte*.

None of us knows just when some word of ours will spark a fire. In that moment, Bill Hull sparked a fire for me. He did not know it then; he may not know it now. But that moment is one of my debts.

I mention this passing incident—and that is all it was—to acknowledge an indebtedness to all those who have sought to inform and inspire me. The responsibility for what I write is mine. The credit for the inspiration behind what I write is theirs.

I take this means of acknowledging a debt. I hope it will encourage those who give themselves to the ministry of teaching.

RALPH L. MURRAY